CONTEMPORARY MENSWEAR

OVER 500 IMAGES

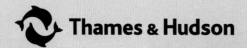

Thames & Hudson

CONTEMPORARY MENSWEAR

A GLOBAL GUIDE TO INDEPENDENT MEN'S FASHION

STEVEN VOGEL
NICHOLAS SCHONBERGER **&**
CALUM GORDON

Dedicated, as always, to Nina, who puts
up with me with a smile, Steven.

Dedicated to my mum, my brother,
and Black Lodges, Nicholas.

Dedicated to my mum and dad. Thank you
for your unwavering support, Calum.

Contemporary Menswear © 2014 Thames & Hudson Ltd,
London

Texts © 2014 Steven Vogel, Nicholas Schonberger
and Calum Gordon

First published in 2014 in paperback in the
United States of America by Thames & Hudson Inc.,
500 Fifth Avenue, New York, New York 10110

thamesandhudsonusa.com

Library of Congress Catalog Card Number 2014932797

ISBN 978-0-500-51759-8

Manufactured in China by Imago Publishing Limited

INTRODUCTION

BY STEVEN VOGEL

Just as my last book, *Streetwear*, was being published in 2007, a notable change in contemporary 'kool kulture' was taking place. Several commentators in my book had mentioned that the trend was towards a cleaner, more mature and preppier look. Unbeknown to most people at the time, a new, all-encompassing trend, one that we now call 'menswear', was to emerge and replace the status of everyone in the last book as the pinnacle of kool kulture. There are several reasons to draw a parallel between the two trends, even if I am the only one lucky enough to have been able to write books about both of them.

The question that arises most commonly, especially from new spectators or those not involved in any sub-cultural movement, is 'what is it?' Or, more precisely in this case, what is menswear? I am genuinely not a fan of definitions when it comes to discussing these trends, yet a few notes are in order – especially since everyone involved in this trend has an opinion on it, as I do, and some of these are more important than others. On a side note, I find the hive mind fascinating when it comes to defining the content and boundaries of these trends. It seems that everyone involved knows what menswear is when we are talking about it without anyone setting out any clear definition.

For argument's sake, contemporary menswear, as portrayed in this book, has been around since the invention of men's fashion. A lot of the protagonists of this trend see themselves as part of a long traditional lineage of careful artisanal craftsmen. To a certain degree, this is true and it does actually apply to some people. Nevertheless, any trend in today's times can be traced back to some event in the past and a somewhat hazy line of relation can always be drawn.

This book is an observation, commentary and compilation of those brands and people who have shaped a new sub-culture, which, unlike many before them, transcends into more than fashion and illustrates a change in lifestyle and attitude.

Poignantly, one does need to ask whether a global early-adopter change in consciousness took place before the rise of menswear, or vice versa. That, however, is to ask which came first, the chicken or the egg.

The fact is that menswear is an expression of a change of modern values, which at this point may or may not reach the mainstream. It goes beyond clothing and has from early on

in its journey touched upon much more than just clothing and trends.

Importantly, menswear, in this vision, encapsulates the idea of quality and traditional craftsmanship and combines this with modern thoughts on sustainability, practicability and life in general. Politics, in the sense of local production of goods, business practice and national vs. international approaches, also comes into play. Menswear is a romantic movement apparently needed in a time of brutal 'realpolitik'.

I mention romanticism because a lot of what defines this trend is based on the marketing idea of a pre-hyper-modern America. Granted, there are drifts within menswear that have little do with 'Americana', but the majority of it is in some way influenced by a romanticized ideal of a manufacturing America. It is romantic because the idea of menswear is not factually based on the reality of the Gilded Age of America, but the image that we like to have of it. This is not meant to be a criticism, though – I have no issue with influential protagonists of any trend propagating values and practices that lead to a slower lifestyle based on quality and an awareness of sustainability.

If menswear, as described here, is more than clothing, then why does this book focus mostly on clothing? Despite the higher moral ground that a lot of menswear claims for itself, it is a trend manifested in clothing and hence a fashion, a business that runs to a different beat than the marketing romance often employed to do just that. It may sound a little harsh, but as it is with essentially every aspirational trend, many factions tag along for the ride and sell you a story that they are not part of.

I do not doubt for one second that a determined core of people believe the aforementioned alternative reality and use the business of menswear as a means to realize that end. In the context of the book you are holding in your hand, though, stripped of all its Instagram-filtered marketing ideas, menswear is part of the global fashion business with all its pros and cons; its idealism won't change any of it.

To get to the knitty gritty of it, contemporary menswear is a popular niche within current men's fashion. A vast majority is inspired by preppy Americana, as championed by popular brands such as Ralph Lauren. Additionally, a healthy dose of American workwear from the likes of Red Wing and reinterpreted by brands such as Levi's Vintage is a necessary ingredient for this cocktail of the modern man. Japanese excellence in design, production and materials, as well as their general obsession with details, is another important factor, along with a degree of Scandinavian modernism and Italian heritage.

Add to this cocktail of fabrics, cuts and materials a large dose of marketing based on the romanticized ideal of the bearded wolf, the artisanal proto-man so comically portrayed in a recent Old Spice commercial, with the business approach of championing the independents and you have almost got to a clearer picture of what menswear is.

The internet is another important aspect in menswear that needs to be mentioned. Without this communications platform, it is hard to imagine that menswear as a niche would have become such an impactful trend within men's fashion. Despite the rugged ideal of a man who would rather communicate by smoke signals, the internet, as with many – if not all – modern trends, played a significant role in propagating the ideals and aesthetic of menswear.

More specifically, the internet was the platform for one of the early instigators of the menswear trend: the streetstyle photographer, most notably the Sartorialist. Irrespective of what many of the burly commentators of menswear may have said about it, the Sartorialist, aka Scott Schuman, made the public aware of the 'Sharped Dressed Man'. Furthermore, it was Mr Schuman's eye, his aesthetic, that paved the way for much of what was to come in menswear.

In addition to the many copycats of the Sartorialist, the usual media landscape of blogs and magazines quickly followed and pushed this new idea of menswear. I think it is important to note that, in the early days, menswear certainly felt a lot smarter than it does today and the initial run by the media on this subject is partly to blame for that. Luckily, rather than copying 1960s Ivy League meets or 1980s Gordon Gekko's *Wall Street*, menswear moved towards the aforementioned proto-grizzly bear man. Not to say that the suit-wearing Patrick Bateman-esque aesthetic doesn't exist anymore, it does, it is simply a part of the larger picture of menswear.

Now that you have read this introduction with an artisanal cup of coffee handmade in your backyard or perhaps with a glorious glass of Scotch made by the virgin sirens of the remote Isles of Japanese Handmade Denim, you must certainly wonder what this book is about.

Essentially, Nicholas Schonberger, Calum Gordon and I selected a number of brands to include in the book that we feel, not just individually but also as a collection, make up the vanguard of menswear. Each and every one of them represents a niche within the niche of menswear. There are two important notes about the selection: brands such as Levi's Vintage Clothing, Red Wing and Ralph Lauren are not included. First we wanted to focus on portraying the notable independent brands, not only to keep within the spirit of menswear, but also because we felt that brands such as those mentioned are so easily accessible that it was fine not to include

them. Their exclusion – make no mistake about this – does not diminish their role in menswear, but for the sake of the idea behind this book we all felt that there was no point in giving them more space than their large marketing budgets already allow them. On that note, there are certain brands not included in this book that should have been. As usual, as soon as you deal with people and their perceptions, it goes beyond the greater good. If a brand is not in here and you think it should be, rest assured that we spoke to them and they either declined to be in the book or simply never answered our messages for reasons unknown to us.

In addition to a selection of representative brands, we also asked a number of very smart, influential and well-respected individuals within the universe of menswear either to comment on important aspects of this niche or, in some cases, tell their own individual story about how they came to menswear and what they make of it.

All in all, I firmly believe you are holding in your hand a great representative snapshot of a hugely fascinating cultural movement and a fashion that encompasses some of the world's greatest creatives and visionaries.

Yours,
Steven Vogel

Page 6: Wood Wood; page 8: Albam Clothing; opposite: The West Is Dead.

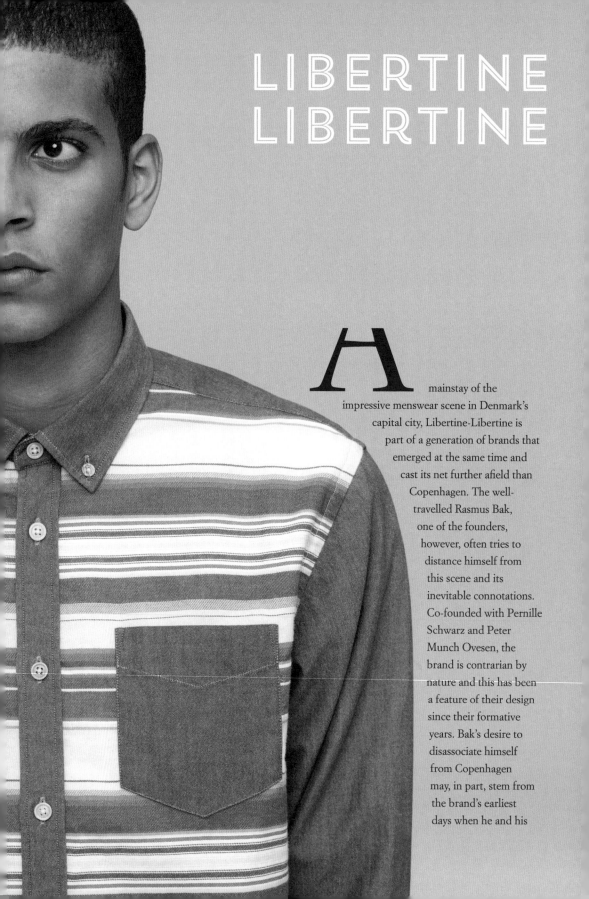

LIBERTINE
LIBERTINE

A mainstay of the
impressive menswear scene in Denmark's
capital city, Libertine-Libertine is
part of a generation of brands that
emerged at the same time and
cast its net further afield than
Copenhagen. The well-
travelled Rasmus Bak,
one of the founders,
however, often tries to
distance himself from
this scene and its
inevitable connotations.
Co-founded with Pernille
Schwarz and Peter
Munch Ovesen, the
brand is contrarian by
nature and this has been
a feature of their design
since their formative
years. Bak's desire to
disassociate himself
from Copenhagen
may, in part, stem from
the brand's earliest
days when he and his

two designers were working out of his apartment. Unlike most brands, Libertine-Libertine didn't initially seek to build a local fan base, but instead used the money it saved on office rent to travel around Europe, reaching out to stockists all over the continent.

Libertine-Libertine's desire to be the antithesis of its surroundings also translated over to the brand's aesthetic. Despite having spent time in the United States flirting with a rock-star lifestyle, Bak made a conscious effort to shun black and skinny jeans: two traits that he viewed as synonymous with Nordic menswear. Instead, Libertine-Libertine combines classic silhouettes with a variety of colours and prints. Its different approach has seen its clothing often being mimicked by its contemporaries, and perhaps that is the greatest testament to the brand's originality.

Opposite, right and following pages: Autumn/Winter 2013/14.

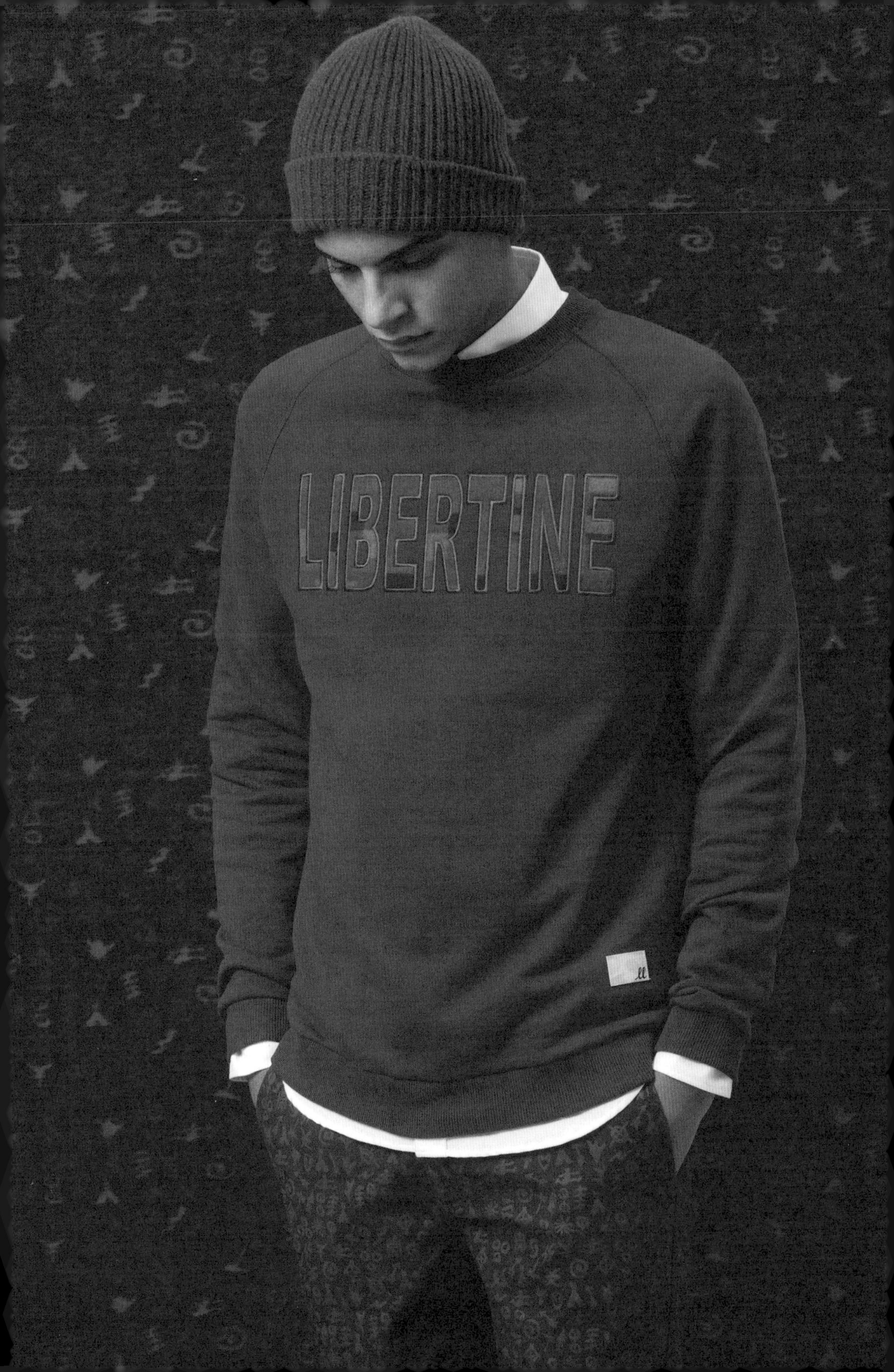
LIBERTINE

ALBAM CLOTHING

The term 'football casual' in modern-day Britain conjures up two sets of sartorial imagery: the halcyon days of wedge haircuts and fast-moving trends that revolved around fresh trainers and imported designer labels and, in stark contrast, the more modern image of rotund, middle-aged men with a penchant for boot-cut jeans and jackets with goggles in the hood. While one form of the 'casual' may not have been the most refined in terms of menswear, it was progressive. The latter example is one mired in stagnation and a desire to re-live memories which have, over the years, become an idealized parody of what they truly were. Why am I talking about casuals? Well, the early success of Albam owes a lot to this once great sub-culture. Or rather it owes something to the more progressive elements of this movement, although most of the people involved wouldn't even dream of calling themselves a casual. Albam has since grown up, but in its formative days it created a buzz with its astonishingly simple, yet much sought-after Fisherman's Cagoule. It may seem crude to attribute the rise of one of London's most influential lifestyle brands to a single jacket and its association with a particular sub-culture – and, of course, this may be an over-simplified version of Albam's early success

– but that single jacket has been paid homage on Casual Connoisseur tees. For many years, Albam had 'casuals10' as a discount code on their website.

Timing is everything. As 'heritage' began to work its way into the psyche of the savvier menswear consumers in the UK, Albam flourished with its 'crafted in England' products. These products were not simply manufactured, they were 'crafted'. Arguably, they encompassed the initial stages of this movement where craftsmanship and origin were king. Albam had a product that seemed genuine at a time when brands would rise or fall based on their perceived authenticity. Beards and wax jackets were most definitely 'in', and Albam executed a distribution scheme that was so tight it may have ensured their longevity. The brand was both honest and desirable: traits that have served it well. When every menswear brand and their dog reinvented themselves, played up their history and tried to cash in on the heritage boom, Albam continued to do what they do best: manufacture honest products in the UK. For all Albam courted the heritage movement, ultimately it allowed consumers to interpret their product in whatever way they saw fit.

Almost a decade has passed since James Shaw and Alastair Rae made their first foray into menswear, working out of a small office above a dentist's surgery. To remain relevant for such a long time is a considerable feat. However, it would be disingenuous to say that Albam has been on a steady trajectory since it was first conceived in 2006: setbacks and slumps are inevitable. This is by no means a slight upon Albam, it's the reality of the menswear game and one that is enshrined upon the wall of the brand's Nottingham design studio. When speaking to Shaw, he gladly acknowledges that it hasn't always run smoothly or to plan, but that's the fun of watching a fresh-faced upstart like Albam mature into a firmly established favourite of the UK's conglomerate of well-dressed folk.

Today, Albam seems to have recaptured the enthusiasm and buzz that first catapulted the company into its early success. Now they've already been round the course, they know the pitfalls to avoid and the direction to take. Inevitably, there will be mistakes along the way, but with three London-based bricks-and-mortar shops and an introduction to a wider European market through Sweden's Très Bien Shop, the future bodes well for Albam. Design-wise Albam has evolved, too: it would be fair to say it is moving with the times while remaining true to its core of functional,

well-made and simple products. While others became caught up in the world of workwear and heritage, Albam evolved and set about making more technical products and fusing them together with the existing basics. As 2012 drew to a close, this shift in focus began to garner a sense of cohesion and reignited the spark that was first lit by a simple wax cotton cagoule.

Preceding pages and opposite:
Autumn/Winter 2012/13.

ENGINEERED GARMENTS

The words heritage and workwear will undoubtedly feature heavily in this book. This is not by design, but reflects the fact that they have defined the last five years in menswear and, arguably, readjusted our attitudes towards clothing in a somewhat more permanent manner. It now seems second nature to look for the qualities of originality and timelessness. Such mannerisms were, for many, less prevalent before this trend emerged, yet they will undoubtedly carry over into whatever people next set their sights upon. While trends come and go, some people truly fall in love with a brand. A cult-like worship ensues and the consumer, not caring about what is alleged to be 'in', is captivated by a certain aesthetic. It is without question very difficult to try to garner such a fan base, never mind define an era in menswear. Engineered Garments, however, has been a flag-bearer for the re-emergence of Americana and has developed fiercely loyal customers in the process. The brand's commitment to military- and workwear-inspired classics is prominent in much of its output, but it has eschewed the tendency of others simply to copy designs of the past. Instead, with Daiki Suzuki at the helm, the brand has moulded an Americana vision of its own.

The story behind the name is one of the most repeated within the whole fashion industry, encapsulating the company's style and ethos in a single anecdote. Engineered Garments took its name from a pattern maker hired to draft the first round of patterns. She claimed that the clothes were not designed, that they were 'engineered' due to the intricacy of each garment. That fateful turn of phrase complemented Suzuki's vision in an ideal marriage of detail and description.

While the brand is inherently American, right down to its production in the garment district of New York, it certainly exudes the Japanese sensibilities of its founder. The detailing, functionality and cut are all reminiscent of the more refined Japanese take on Americana. It is, as he describes it, his own take on modern sportswear. Since its inception in 1999, each collection has been grounded yet beautiful, a far cry from more conceptual, artistic fashion, yet beautiful nonetheless. Engineered Garments is an amalgamation of Suzuki's interests and hobbies; there is no overriding theme. For all its foundation in traditional work and military garments, there are nuances of Ivy League prep and vintage surf vibes woven throughout each seasonal offering.

While current interests inform his collections, it was Suzuki's youth that, to some extent, formed his vision for what Engineered Garments should look like. In an interview with his protégé Shinya Hasegawa in 2013, Suzuki reminisced about how the 1970s moulded his design nuances and his outlook. 'There was a lot of American pride back then, due to the 200th anniversary of the nation, and you could see a real dedication to American clothing made in America. I was also really interested in how American clothing was rugged and only fitted well after being worn for a while – clothing like jeans and t-shirts that changed bit by bit with each wear and wash, until they were totally different from when you first bought them. This type of clothing was really unique, and striking to clothing connoisseurs all over the world. Also, at that time, in the 1970s, the thought of Made in the USA conjured all of these dream-like images of places far away, y'know, romantic notions of California and New York.

Looking back at this image I'd formed of America when I was young, I realize it still influences my designs today. I definitely have a nostalgia for American products "Made in USA" – and that forms the basis for Engineered Garments, at least in part.'

Today, life looks pretty rosy for the man behind the clothes. With five shops in Japan and a store in New York, which combines his own brand with an impressive roster from Nepenthes, his business is healthy. It is the pay-off for the daily grind of turning up two hours before and leaving two hours after all his other employees. At the weekends Suzuki rises at five o'clock to go surfing and by one o'clock he'll be back in his office, often working until he falls asleep. It is an obsession and a passion that consumes much of his time. The results, ironically, produce garments that look effortless.

Despite humbly describing himself as merely 'a guy who used to work at a clothing store and just happened to get into designing', the longevity and popularity of his work is testament to his ability to craft a unique identity for his brand.

Preceding pages: Daiki Suzuki, brand founder and creative director, and some of his products; opposite: the brand's studio, based in New York's garment district.

DENIM DEMON

Denim is perhaps the most commonly worn and commonly misunderstood fabric in contemporary menswear. Its history in both fashion and workwear is long and heavy. The various styles are testament to an ebb and flow in popularity, but one thing is constant: jeans are simply part of our lives.

Denim also connects with consumer interest in heritage,

workwear and manufacture. This is in no small part due to the great number of Japanese repro brands and their undying desire for authenticity. Through those brands – Samurai, Flathead and the like – niche interest in looms, fabrics and dyes has exploded. The denim labels founded in the last decade balance a unique blend of historical authenticity and local articulation of the classic jean.

Stockholm-based Denim Demon operates under a simple and admirable mission: 'to protect and to nurse the blue jeans heritage'. Founders and brothers Oskar Sommarlund and Anton Olsson proceed with a reverence and love for the history of their chosen product. Their personal twist is an incorporation of their own Sami native northern Scandinavian heritage, which informs their craft-focused design.

'It's easy to be inspired looking at Sami handicraft,' says Sommarlund. 'Take a knife, which can take anything between three weeks and six months to create. A lot of time, effort and passion is put into this little thing. This is what made us start in the denim business as well. We want to create something more than just a product, a complete story with all our garments, which adds value.'

Part of the storytelling has involved finding the perfect wash. In this endeavour, Sommarlund and Olsson engineered a delightfully interesting project. Seven people from northern Sweden, representatives of Sami culture, were given raw jeans to wear for six months. The jeans were then shipped to Japan to be replicated, and the results were both stunning in appearance and exciting as a cultural project.

'This has also helped us to get closer to our heritage – our grandmother was Sami, and we made ourselves learn so much about it,' says Sommarlund. 'We are proud of our story, and want to tell the world about it.'

The wear-out project proved denim's transition from American workwear to global icon. With Denim Demon there is no doubting the understanding of tradition in the garment. But there is the added benefit of seeing how that mutates and grows over time and across space. The brand represents the potential of denim to explore rooted, direct influences removed from the tried-and-true image of the American West.

Opposite: Denim Demon campaign images shot in Sweden; overleaf: Autumn/Winter 2011/12.

FOLK

It is a truism of British fashion that nearly all talent will eventually drift southwards towards the seductive beckoning of London. Understandably, Folk's founder Cathal McAteer was no exception. While the Cumbernauld-born designer first honed his skills in Ichi Ni San, Glasgow's seminal retail space, handling the wares of designers such as Dries Van Noten, somewhat inevitably there was not enough in Glasgow to hold his interest and McAteer found himself in London, where he worked for the likes of Nicole Farhi and YMC. In 2001, he summoned all that he had learned and ploughed it into forming a brand of his own. It was a brand that stood out from the norm of heavily branded clothes which were typical of the new millennium. McAteer chose to focus on subtle details such as buttons made from crushed coconut shells or hand-woven Japanese cord trims.

The Folk aesthetic has changed little over the years; each collection is built from the same core principles that informed the first collection. What has changed, however, are the nuances of menswear consumers in terms of both age and tastes. Those who once pined for limited edition graphic tees now seek a greater degree of refinement and elegance.

Folk provide this. It is, however, in the attention to such minute details in which Folk sets itself apart from its competitors in an industry that has at times become all too obsessed with providing 'classics with a twist'. In reality, there were few independents approaching menswear design from such a contemporary angle before Folk. According to McAteer himself, their approach to each garment is encapsulated by Charles Eames when he said, 'the details are not the details, they make the design.'

You were born in Cumbernauld, perhaps not the most creatively inspiring place in Scotland – what was it that first sparked your interest in clothes? For the most part, it seems that kids of that era had only two routes which got them into designer brands – music or football…

Football was my real passion; I still love it, though for me it showed no direct route to fashion. I was really into dressing up and looking different, but it was only when I walked into Ichi Ni San, aged 15, and Stephen, one of the owners, asked me to model for them that I really got seduced by it all. Shortly after that they kindly asked me to work Saturdays, and from there I experimented heavily with all the wares.

After a brief stint in Brussels, you found yourself in London working for Nicole Farhi and YMC before you founded your own brand. Had it always been an ambition to start Folk? What was the catalyst for starting the brand?

While working to learn and earn, I was assisting my then girlfriend Zakee Shariff, a really talented designer/printmaker/artist. We travelled to Japan together and on one such trip the hosts asked, 'When will you do menswear?' This hadn't been the plan: I wasn't ready but, always wanting to please (myself usually first), at their request I started to make my first pieces. Using the south island of Japan as a place to experiment with the Folk style, it was not until two years later that I would bring it to London for the first time.

How long were you based in Japan while creating Folk and how did it inform the brand's aesthetic?

I wasn't based there, but the first customers were there. It was initially sold in Fukuoka, in a store called Dice & Dice. The first five seasons we purely designed and sold in Japan. The only bits that made it to the UK were for friends. Through visiting many times, there was most certainly influence from the Japanese market. The people, and the way they put their stuff together, are strong – meticulous yet refined. It's a great place for any aspiring creative to go and just look at people and things.

Preceding pages, below and opposite: Spring/Summer 2014.

How hard is it to convey Folk's unique detailing and special fabrics in a world where a large percentage of purchases are online? From the Folk pieces I've owned, pictures on the internet have never done the garments true justice. It must be a constant challenge…

It is, and we try to find better ways of presenting ourselves online, but we don't lose sleep over it. We are a design company that prides itself on the great product we make. If we keep with this attitude, we won't compromise the heart of what we are.

A lot of your fabrics are woven specifically for Folk and buttons are custom-made. What is it that drives you to go to such lengths when creating collections?

In the beginning there were such heavy restrictions on where we could make, on what fabrics we could buy, which often meant buying from stock houses and making in the East End of London. We spent a lot of time enhancing the look of the garment with hand finishes, old buttons and drawing lines on inside seams to add some warmth and care to the whole garment.

This ethos has remained: it's part of what we do. Nothing is off limits with regards to doing our own thing: buttons, fabrics, threads and laces, lights and bags, tables and ceramics.

Folk is the creative outlet for Scottish designer Cathal McAteer, centre right.

With such a labour-intensive fabric process and burgeoning seasonal collections, is it hard to stay inspired and remain creative in order to put out new collections every six months? Where do you draw your inspiration from?

Honestly, it's not hard to stay inspired as we love what we do and there is so much more we can do. There is also an inner confidence that we have gained through roughing out some tough times and through 10 years of Folk.

The design team takes influence from all over. Art is a strong influence, especially in London. Most recently we looked at the lauded architect Oscar Niemeyer, juxtaposing the massive sprawl of favelas and the pattern and colour they showcase.

You currently have four men's shops, three in London and one in Amsterdam. Why Amsterdam? Am I also correct in saying there was once a Folk shop in Munich? Even with retail locations, Folk seems to avoid the obvious, or stereotypical…

Yes, Amsterdam was down to doing well and the shop owner asking us to do it with him. It was an easy one to say yes to. There was a store in Munich, yes. Again it was an idea we could act out, but I think an amount of naivety and courage did not make a recipe for success.

With regards to shop locations, here in London at Lambs Conduit Street we are very happy and the other locations are great too. We don't go out of our way to be off the wall, it's more that this is where we were drawn to by our needs and vision. Lambs Conduit Street is now our home and many have followed since our arrival – this has created a real destination street.

Again, it's part of who we are – to try to find locations and shop units that feel right. Shepherd Street was one such store in an off-beat part of town, which is home to the original Curzon Cinema, the former Tiddy Dolls (Rolling Stones fans should know the stories), the best French restaurant in London, an infamous trade in the oldest profession in the world and us. It's got character and charm and no other stores like ours.

What do you have in store for the future? Am I correct in saying you've dabbled in furniture? I know Charles Eames is a great inspiration to you and the brand.

I hope the future brings growth in our women's business, as well as the expansion of the tailoring we have been selling, which looks strong. Perhaps more stores and more categories.

Procreating should always be on the agenda. We have a young-ish group, so we expect many little ones to arrive over the coming years… no pressure.

Oh, and having fun while working is a must. We are not exactly Yvon Chouinard, but we should all take a little from the fine example he sets.

Elbe Lealman, the head designer at Folk, is maturing into one of the very best around. I think she has a lot more in the tank.

'The details are not the details, they make the design' – and the Eames work is undoubtedly exceptional. It was this quote that really stuck with us, as it is part of us here.

Ceramics for December this year. And lights… We recently lit the artists' bar at the Hay-on-Wye literary festival. With furniture, too, there is something there but it's in the development stage. Like in our clothing, buttons, fabrics, etc., we don't go to the furniture shop to buy a bench, we design our own and have it made.

Away from clothing and design work, what interests you?

Having fun with my family and friends is generally top of the list, particularly as summer draws to a close. Hampstead Heath is fantastic in autumn; running around with the kids and trying to fit in one last swim before it's too cold.

Also trying to see, read or listen to as much stuff by way of art, literature and music as possible. It's always never enough. Although this year Glastonbury was my best ever; the Block 9 area smashed it with the best music I have heard for a long time.

Aside from Folk, what other brands do you wear or have an appreciation for? As someone who goes to great lengths to create unique fabrics and garments, there must be peers who you are proud to sit alongside.

Dries Van Noten is duly number one. APC is a great example of a company that has thrived, and we feel proud and comfortable to be put in their bracket. In the newer world Our Legacy is very nice and the guys there are dope and worth a visit – Friday night in Stockholm!

Opposite: Autumn/Winter 2013/14.

RETAIL

by Arthur Chmielewski

WWW.HAVENSHOP.CA

Arthur Chmielewski is the co-founder/owner of the store Haven in Canada, with shops in Vancouver, Edmonton and Toronto. Haven is one of the best retailers on a global scale in terms of brand presentation, originality and content. The brand has not only defined contemporary menswear as we understand it, but more importantly continuously adds their own twist.

\X/ hen my brother Daniel and I opened our first clothing boutique in 2006, the retail landscape was very different from how it currently is today. During that time, the sneaker and streetwear craze was at its peak. It seemed as if new brands and shops were emerging almost daily, and it felt as if those who were involved or in the know were protected from the general consumer masses and corporations. We were happy in our modest streetwear sub-culture bubble.

Fast forward to the present and the marketplace has changed drastically. With the rise and popularity of blogs and social media, information travels instantly; consumers now have access to information at their fingertips. And the way they shop had to evolve to follow suit. E-commerce has become a multi-billion dollar industry with a plethora of strong online shops offering comprehensive selections for every category, from streetwear and contemporary menswear, to high fashion and everything in between – all with competitive pricing. Virtually every relevant retail operation, small or large, has a web store component to it, with a few key players dominating the market share in every category.

Existing solely as a bricks and mortar is becoming increasingly difficult as the consumer pot is shrinking. E-commerce retailers who are able to provide larger product selections and more exclusive offerings at competitive prices are swallowing up the bulk of the market share. As a result of this emerging online landscape, the traditional boutique business model now faces new challenges. Boutiques generally pride themselves on their unique product, exclusive brand lists and curated retail environments. However, with the ability to shop from any boutique in any corner of the globe at any time, the importance of regional exclusivity has been greatly diminished. Online purchasing has made it easy to procure the latest 'exclusive' release. Consumers are becoming savvier, and they know it's often more affordable and less time-consuming to order online than support their local boutique.

As retail channels evolve and converge, so must boutiques. With more and more brands choosing to sell their collections directly to consumers via their own e-commerce platforms, the competition has become fierce. The seasonal selling windows have become shorter, and the margins have become smaller. Retailers are now competing directly with the very brands that sell to them.

The challenge for independent boutiques currently becomes how to distinguish themselves from one another. How do they set themselves apart? Boutiques must find new ways to become influencers in their own right. The game has changed and the most successful are now the ones who have integrated all aspects of their business to fit the digital playing field, while still offering an outstanding physical experience. Retailers must consider restructuring their roles not only to operate as resellers, but also as producers – producers of exclusive in-house product(s), exceptional online content and editorials, well-executed collaborations along with reliable sources of information for their consumers. Only then can they maintain their relevance in an oversaturated and highly competitive marketplace.

By becoming a producer, they shift the influencing power back in their favour. They create exclusivity and unique content for themselves, with the choice to sell to as few or as many as is beneficial to them. On top of that, by cutting out the middleman, boutiques are able to achieve greater margins or traffic, with a more vertically integrated business model. However, when all is said and done, this is not an easy task. It involves a very talented and dedicated team of creative individuals with leaders who can think outside of the box, advancing the company in the right direction.

To replicate a formula from the past is no longer relevant: the bar has now been raised significantly. In order to establish a foothold as an independent retailer today, you must approach the market with a strong and original vision of what differentiates your company from the competition, and how to communicate this message effectively with your customer base and media.

When developing as an independent retailer, it is key to figure out what your company stands for, who your target market is, what niche you are trying to fill, what your aesthetic is and how you translate that into your retail and online environments, and how your web presence works hand in hand to elevate your customers' experience. These are all questions that a retailer must be able to answer.

Consider not just launching with a strong e-commerce presence but perhaps vertically integrating your company with a well thought out in-house line or strong collaborative products with key brands to set yourself apart. In a few years, this will no longer be an option but rather a necessity – parallel to how maintaining a strong e-commerce operation is increasingly important today. As we converge into a highly competitive global marketplace, these will be key factors that decide the longevity of the independent boutique.

Preceding pages and opposite: Haven's bricks-and-mortar store in Toronto, Canada.

GARBSTORE

Garbstore is the brainchild of English designer Ian Paley. The brand is the culmination of Paley's ideas and experiences of menswear. A clothing obsessive from an early age, he took the traditional route of studying fashion at university before, like many of his peers, first breaking into the industry at Paul Smith. Subsequently, Paley was part of a trio who set up the pioneering brand One True Saxon. Eventually he sold up, but he had gained a reputation and a core following that loved the utilitarian aspects of his design and the attention to detail for which his clothes were renowned.

After One True Saxon, Paley set up Garbstore as a brand, but also as a retail destination in London. Stylistically, Garbstore incorporates similar elements of workwear and sportswear in a very contemporary manner. It would be hard to categorize the brand aesthetically and perhaps more accurate to say that its emphasis on quality design and interesting textiles is of much greater importance than attempting to label Garbstore. At the heart of the brand is a quality product which will be appreciated by consumers at the London and Los Angeles bricks-and-mortar stores.

Opposite: Garbstore's London shop; overleaf: The Notting Hill outlet in West London provides a variety of lifestyle and womenswear goods, alongside its menswear offering.

LAVENHAM

Lavenham is a brand with genuine history and heritage, spanning over four decades, yet it would not have been considered a 'menswear' brand until relatively late in its existence. Founded in 1969, the company originally specialized in nylon horse quilts. In 1972 it reapplied its expertise in making fine quilts to the realms of outerwear. The brand sat alongside Barbour as the go-to clothier of any ardent countryphile or horse rider. Complementing its quintessential British designs is its commitment to only using manufacturers within the UK. This move has not only served to ensure excellent quality, but has also positioned the brand as one of great British repute. To this day, the company endeavours to make the most of British resources and materials – a refreshing notion against a backdrop of Made in China pseudo-heritage brands. Indeed, it is brands such as Lavenham that have been torchbearers for the gradual resurgence of British textile manufacturing in recent years.

As much as the quilted jackets of Lavenham were traditionally the domain of the countryside-dwelling upper classes, they were not confined to that audience. Rather, the quilted jacket found itself being sported by football casuals who, in a manner similar to how many streetwear brands have made their fortune, reappropriated the look from the wealthy and gave it a new lease of life. Perhaps, had it not been for that once progressive movement, the quilt would have remained in the wardrobes of horse riders and no one else. Lavenham, however, saw the jackets being exposed to a wider audience and consequently embraced the idea. By 2011, the quilt jacket had officially become a mainstream 'trend', yet Lavenham retained its integrity by not deviating from what it had been doing in order to chase the money. The company simply continued to make quality quilts in the UK and such integrity arguably safeguarded its future, in particular the ever-expanding menswear line, from burning out and losing credibility.

Perhaps it was a stroke of good luck that heritage exploded in the way that it did. Lavenham's Made in Britain product, which had existed for decades prior to such demand for authenticity, appealed to many European and Japanese brands who sought to infuse their street-informed design sensibilities with the company's traditional techniques and styles. The result was collaborations with the likes of Norse Projects, Beams and Sophnet for their 10th anniversary collection. Quite simply, they had knowledge

and techniques that could not be acquired overnight: they were the result of over 30 years of manufacturing quilted products in Britain. While such collaborations allowed brands to capitalize on Lavenham's expertise, the company gained exposure to previously untapped markets, taking their version of British heritage global. Lavenham, in turn, embraced this recognition and delved further into the realms of menswear, experimenting with new styles and forming

collections that could hold their own with other menswear brands.

Particularly within fashion, the company you keep is vital to how you are perceived. Lavenham have positioned themselves in a way that will ensure longevity while they continue to refine and redefine their menswear collections. Each collection has, and will inevitably be based on, quilts, yet they have shown they are adept in other departments and capable of creating lines that have a far-reaching appeal.

Preceding pages: Spring/Summer 2013; opposite and above: the increasingly comprehensive range from the master quilt-makers.

OUTLIER

Necessity drives innovation. A pair of trousers that you can ride in on a bike but are stylish enough for everyday wear may seem superfluous, but our hurried lives suggest differently. It is not the trousers as such that are a necessity, but the small things that make everyday life easier. Outlier provides such innovative clothing with a focus on making our lives marginally more comfortable and stress-free.

The idea for Outlier was first sparked by the need for trousers and shirts that could withstand daily commutes on a bike while still retaining an element of style. A first-world problem, undoubtedly, but it was one that Tyler Clemens and Abe Burmeister endeavoured to solve.

Right: Outlier ultralight blazer; overleaf: Autumn/Winter 2011/12.

Ever since Outlier sold its first pair of trousers in Australia, it has operated strictly as an internet business. Since 2008, the brand's two founders have been able to quit their jobs, neither of which were in fashion, in order to focus on the company. Their refreshing approach to clothing has spurned not only an interesting business model, but also practical, wearable clothing.

THE WEST IS DEAD

The rugged terrain of northern Montana has never been mistaken for a fashion hub. Still, it is the type of locale that inspires Ralph Lauren's RRL line and produces the archival photographs that get the Tumblr crowd overexcited. Far removed from all this hype, it was here in the upper Rocky Mountains

that Will Cheng and Kaelen McCrane decided to start their label, The West is Dead, in 2011. Neither one had a background in the garment industry, but they shared an undying passion for things that work and a healthy reverence for the craft element of traditional manufacturing. As such, they have slowly built a brand that speaks to historical influences – without resulting in costume – and champions good quality, durable contemporary clothing, shunning mass production.

Painter Charles Marion Russell is an inspiration to you, as is the state of Montana. Tell me about how your experiences in the 'Big Sky State' helped shape your brand.
WC: I think our experiences living in Montana and working outside the fashion industry gave us a unique insight into the fashion world. We're less influenced by trends and fashion because, honestly, we don't know what's trending. We don't have

a formal design process with mood boards or colour stories. Our process for design and development really happens in the middle stages of production. Many of our design elements and colours are born from mistakes that we make. We think something will look good a certain way and sometimes it gets messed up and comes out completely different and much better.

You moved to Los Angeles because that is where you felt you could make clothing in the United States. What were the biggest initial hurdles?
Moving from Montana to Los Angeles was a huge personal adjustment. After that, the biggest initial hurdle was trying to comprehend the immense process of manufacturing clothes. There are so many steps in making a garment and, for the most part, none of the steps is connected to any other: it is a series of many separate stages. The clothes travel through a completely fractured network of

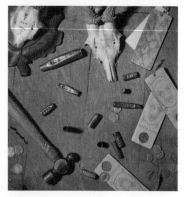

contractors. They don't communicate with each other: they each do one step in the process and it's up to us to make sure everyone does their part. The really tricky thing is that every category of clothing takes a completely different chain of contractors to produce, meaning the people who make our jeans are not the same people who make our t-shirts. We have a completely different supply chain and production channel for each type of clothing. This is one reason why producing clothes in the United States is so difficult and expensive.

What is your take on the heritage trend? Obviously, you're working after the hype has (thankfully) died. What is the trend's lasting legacy?

I'm a big fan of vintage things. I like learning the back story and the nostalgia, and I love studying vintage clothes. But I'm not a heritage purist. I think the heritage trend went wrong by trying to make exact replicas of the most obscure articles of clothing people could dig up. The fact is, vintage clothes were often built solely with function in mind. If you were a miner and you needed jeans with a 24-inch bottom opening so you could pull them over your boots, that's practical: when you put that same pair of pants on someone today, it can just look silly. Our goal is to make contemporary clothes using heritage methods. By staying true to a vintage manufacturing process we capture just enough of the heritage look, but we stop short of pocket watches and penny farthing bicycles. I think the trend's lasting legacy will be that it changed some people's preference for disposable clothes. It seems like now people want one pair of jeans or one jacket that is their favourite and they want to wear it forever, rather than wanting one of everything in every colour, at a price cheap enough to give it away in a year.

Pages 54–55: Spring 2011; preceding pages: Autumn/ Winter 2011/12; left and opposite: Autumn/Winter 2011/12.

NIGEL CABOURN

A legend in the field of heritage brands, the much lauded Nigel Cabourn has been in the business of reinterpreting vintage clothing for contemporary audiences for over four decades. A maverick in terms of design and yet a stickler for detail, you could forgive Cabourn for exuding an air of infallibility, although he is the first to acknowledge how much he owes to the tight-knit, familial nature of his business and the enthusiasm of his small but dedicated workforce. Speaking candidly about 'the power of having young people around you', Cabourn recounted how his much copied Cameraman jacket came to prominence: 'When Drew, my head of sales, joined me six years ago I had 25 Cameraman jackets in the cupboard, which we were stuck with from 2003. He was a young man and he said, "Nige, I've always loved that jacket", but we didn't sell it first time round. He started selling them to his mates, so we brought it back and made half a million on that jacket alone that season.' A jacket that had been consigned to a dusty cupboard was thus reissued to become a consistent bestseller. This flexibility and willingness to return to the past is characteristic of Cabourn, who has spent years perfecting the art of rummaging around for old jackets in order to give them a new lease of life.

We visited Cabourn in his office near Newcastle in England, where a backdrop of vintage books and prints sets the tone for our post-lunch interview. He recalled, 'My mother and father were pretty easy-going. Initially, I wanted to be a journalist and write about football. And I actually wanted to be a professional goalkeeper until I realized when I got to sixteen or seventeen that you had to be totally dedicated. I liked to go out and party and drink and chase girls, so the commitment wasn't there to be a footballer, but certainly the commitment was there to do something in fashion.' Between 1967 and 1971, Cabourn attended fashion college in Newcastle and the city became a source of inspiration for Cricket, the first label he founded. 'From fashion college I was totally inspired to make my own product and actually get my coats on the backs of people, and that's what I did. By 1971 I had people wearing my stuff. I designed everything and got it manufactured all locally in Newcastle. So not only had I designed it, but I also got the patterns cut and was producing it, making it, selling it to local shops.'

Unlike his current collections, Cricket was much more of its time: 'It was all based on the pop stars of the late 1960s. In the late 1960s, there were no niche brands: companies like the one I was starting didn't exist.' Today, the epicentre of the iconic Nigel Cabourn brand resides just off the high street of a small town near Newcastle. To get there, you have to walk past Cabourn's family home and through a gate to the back garden, where you find a small two-storey building housing the label's offices.

While much of Cabourn's design inspiration relies on the vintage pieces that he avidly collects on his travels, the uncompromising nature of Tyneside's often dreary weather provides a perfect backdrop for a brand that is best known for its British-made outerwear. Cabourn also travels extensively. 'I travel four months of the year,' he chirps with the enthusiasm of a child heading out on a school field trip. 'I'm privy to all the best places, and if you travel to interesting places, you pick up interesting things, whether it's vintage clothes or books or seeing a famous exhibition. Inevitably, if I go to Tokyo or Sydney, or anywhere in the world, there will be something on that's really inspiring.' It is the juxtaposition of these influences – his roots in the north-east of England

Preceding pages: The Mallory Jacket; above and opposite: Nigel Cabourn and his showroom featuring his Autumn/Winter 2013/14 collection.

and his globe-trotting lifestyle – that accounts for the Nigel Cabourn aesthetic.

Cabourn's love of all things old has been a near-constant theme in his designs for over three decades. While vintage garments always held his interest, it was an introduction to the Clignancourt flea market in Paris by a certain Paul Smith, a former employee of Cabourn's, that shaped the label's style as we know it today. 'Although I had an interest in vintage in the late 1960s,' Cabourn says, 'it evolved, and as I got older, I met people. I realized by about 1978

that there were stores and flea markets in Paris which actually specialized in vintage things.' This exposure to a variety of designs, detailing and styles inspired Cabourn to take elements from them and incorporate different combinations into new looks. 'I first found a British military jacket with a button and tape idea – a slide button – in 1979. Between

1979 and 1981, I made that idea so famous. The idea was copied by everybody, from the likes of Stone Island to Chevignon, but I reckon I was there before all of them.'

'I'm very inspired by vintage fabrics,' Cabourn continues. 'Most of the old British fabrics either don't exist or they're very expensive to make because they're high quality and these mills aren't producing very much. On top of that, today manufacturing is a dying trade in this country.' Despite such difficulties, Cabourn insists on an attention to detail and craftsmanship that set his garments apart. 'You can't really make a cheap Cabourn product,' he points out. 'These copiers' – of whom there are many – 'always do it badly.'

One of the ironies of the brand is that, despite its reliance on traditional craftsmanship, Cabourn also champions the benefits of new technology. Although he is quite frank in admitting that he personally doesn't use a computer at all, he has every single garment designed on one of four Apple computers that face the entrance to his garden workshop. 'I start off with a vintage piece and photograph it. We might use three vintage pieces just for part of the idea for the jacket. Then we draw out the parts of the details and build it like a building on the computer – that's how we do it.'

The tight-knit Nigel Cabourn workforce has designed in this way for a little under two decades with great success: 'I had two guys, Nick and Gary, who helped me get into computers so we could design through them. Silicon Graphics was one of the first computers that built creatively – all of *Jurassic Park* was created on Silicon Graphics – and I had one fifteen years ago when most designers didn't even know about it. I spent £100,000 on it. Can you believe about fifteen years ago I paid £100,000 for a computer? And I couldn't really afford it. I bought it with HP over three years, but it's the best thing I ever did. That was how I developed our design process. We realized we could take vintage pieces, photograph them, put them into the computer and then join them together with other vintage garments. I reckon we almost invented that system. It's very technical. Even though I can't use a computer, I understand the benefits of it.'

A pioneer in more ways than one, Cabourn also paved the way for British designers in the Japanese market: 'I've had a business relationship with the Japanese since 1979. There was nobody other than myself, the big brand names and Margaret Howell who I can remember in Japan in those days.' British fashion is a small world, with everyone's careers seemingly interwoven. The success and influence of Nigel Cabourn and Margaret Howell, long-time compatriots in the field of niche brands, paved the way for many other British designers to succeed in Japan. As the first two British designers to break into Japan, apart from heritage heavyweights Aquascutum and Burberry, they opened the door for the likes of Paul Smith and Vivienne Westwood.

The influence of Japan on the Nigel Cabourn brand is arguably as important as that of vintage clothing: while vintage style informs its design, Japan has driven its business. 'I stopped Cricket and became a designer in 1983. I'd got right into the Japanese market from the late 1970s and they were doing very well with what I was making. The Japanese said, "Look, we really need you to have a name – in Japan we need names." Of course, in that period you didn't have any real names. Margaret [Howell] and I were really the first two brand names. Even though we were very small, we were pioneers.'

Cabourn readily acknowledges that much of his success is owed to the Japanese. It is an unexpected characteristic of the market for niche brands that, while fashion-conscious Brits are forever seeking out little-known Japanese labels for their exclusivity and craftsmanship, Japanese consumers are equally enamoured with British heritage brands, whatever the price tag. Cabourn offers his own insight into this phenomenon, based on his understanding of Japanese history: 'The Japanese have their own

history, but they love American history and they love British history. They really appreciate it. The Japanese consumer is very different from the UK consumer. They're very hip. A Japanese guy will spend half his money on clothes. If he earns 20,000 a year, he'll spend 10,000 of it on clothes. That's how they are; they have different values. They're not so bothered about buying a house like we are; they're quite happy to spend it on Cameraman jackets. A lot of this culture comes from the uncertainty that they live with. Japan has been hit by some enormous earthquakes. In 1923 the whole of Tokyo was completely flattened, so they're brought up with that and have learned that life might be more for living rather than saving.'

While the appreciation of the craft involved in a Nigel Cabourn jacket is not limited to Japan, Japanese sales have certainly given the brand a solid footing over the years. In Europe and the United States, the Cabourn Authentic collection is also a much revered mainstay of the menswear scene, so much so that the first bricks-and-mortar Nigel Cabourn store outside of Japan will be opening in London.

Cabourn's enthusiasm for his label is refreshing: it truly seems like a labour of love for him. There is no ego whatsoever in this man who dons a £3,000 cashmere coat simply to cross the road for a cup of coffee. The passion he exudes is almost tangible, yet there is humility too and a real respect for those who have helped make the Nigel Cabourn operation so successful.

'I think I have loyal customers because I stick to my roots,' Cabourn says. 'My main thing is that I don't change. I don't do trends. I can't look at any trends on the computer because I don't use one. For me, design is about the heritage, about a story and the quality, British quality, that always has a story to it. There's much more to a Cabourn product. It's not just a product – it's a history and has a story to go with it – and that's how we've built the brand.'

Nigel Cabourn's vintage shoe collection.

YUKETEN

W hile Yuki Matsuda was relatively unknown to most in the pre-heritage boom, the Osaka-born designer had been championing classic Americana footwear and luggage since 1985. The brand is one that has undoubtedly been aided by the growing desire among many men interested in fashion effectively to shun it.

Quality is of paramount importance to Matsuda, who still insists on using American-based manufacturers. In a world where the term 'artisan' has been used to the point of redundancy in order to elevate the perceived quality of products, Yuketen is one of a select few whose authenticity cannot be doubted. Generally, a pair of handmade Yuketen shoes can take anywhere between 96 to 120 hours to make. It is a small sacrifice for Matsuda, who can be safe in the knowledge that the owner will likely have years of wear from them.

Founded by Meg Company in 1989, Yuketen began life as a moccasin-focused concept and subsequently developed into an all-encompassing footwear and accessory range. Located in the shoe-manufacturing stronghold of Maine in the United States, Matsuda's brand has been one of the most prominent within menswear in recent years. His heritage-led styles, coupled with a preference for unexpected fabrics, have allowed the brand to flourish, rather than being bogged down by repetition.

In recent years, Yuketen's output has been complemented by the founding of Meg Company's Monitaly, a menswear line based on similar principles and aesthetics.

Opposite: Yuketen's shoes are all manufactured in the United States; overleaf: Spring/Summer 2013.

MENSWEAR: A LOVE AFFAIR

by Minya Quirk

WWW.BPMW-AGENCY.COM

Minya Quirk is a partner in BPMW, New York, an agency that works with a number of high-profile brands such as Mark McNairy, C.E, Gloverall, Head Porter, Lightning Bolt, Norse and Shades of Grey also produces (capsule), possibly the most important trade show within the contemporary menswear realm. Quirk's insight and foresight into all aspects of fashion and the industry behind it certify her as one of the key protagonists on a global scale.

M

y affair with menswear perhaps began on the day, some time in the late 1980s, when my mother and I bought a seersucker suit from the 44th Street Brooks Brothers store for my father. My dad was a Brooks Brothers man through and through – three-button navy or tweed jackets, always called a 'sport coat' – worn with cords in the 1970s, khakis in the 1980s and any variation of buttoned collar shirt, also from Brooks Brothers. It was Ralph Lauren for weekends and after work. Never Chaps, never Dockers, no athletic brands, just Polo. Dad liked short shorts of the tennis variety, which proved hard to find anywhere through the saggy late 1980s and 1990s. He wore vintage ones for years – white, navy or khaki coloured. There was an L.L. Bean sweater or two thrown into the mix, and a big shearling coat that lasted only until about 1982. Adidas sneakers (then to New Balance later in life) and single monkstrap shoes from Churches, only brown. It was a song that remained the same until a slight aberration in his shopping and wardrobe habits occurred, when Banana Republic opened in the Danbury Mall near his work as an in-house ad man at Union Carbide in Connecticut, some time in the mid-1980s. The cargo pockets of those photojournalist vests and the brushed twill shirts with epaulettes, coupled with the store's faux elephant foot stools, must have spoken to an affinity for Hemingway or some part of his personal masculine image: he'd come home with lots of shirts, sometimes five at a time. Giddy with a shopping high, he'd dump the goods out on the kitchen table while my sister, mom and I would look at him, then at each other with a shrug. Only a few of those pieces remained in constant rotation over the years, but some did play nicely with the Brooks Brothers tweeds. Dad loved to get dressed for parties, maybe a purple tie for kicks. 'It's the colour of royalty!' he'd belt out. 'Does your old dad look terrific or what?' He was confident and sure. Fashion – always a uniform within bounds of acceptability for a Cambridge man, a Yankee

through and through, a bookish charmer who practised Zen Buddhism and loved a drink – was fun for him. But never worth too much effort or seriousness. When my mother and I, breathless for how cute he'd look, unzipped the garment bag to reveal that seersucker suit, my father let out a guffaw and furrowed his brow. 'Why you and your mother are under some impression that I'd want to look like a fucking icecream man, I can't understand,' he said. Or something to that effect. The icecream man bit being the point. In menswear there were rules. The suit went back.

But every man is different. My husband, perhaps the sartorial opposite of my father, grew up in pre-gentrified Clinton Hill in the Fort Greene section of Brooklyn, a Gen Xer with a knack for inventiveness and a penchant for peacocking. For black males, especially in New York City, through history and at any given time, the fashion rules are different from how they are for anyone else, anywhere else. Looking fresh is key. Clean is the word. Pressed and dressed to impress. My mother-in-law tells tales of my husband heading to Prince Street with hard-earned cash saved to splurge on a pair of orange goose-down space boots from Henry Lehr. He was flipping the same Brooks Brothers button-down shirts that my father had (but was probably opting for the Crazy Shirts, which were, of course, too crazy for dad), maybe with Andrew Marc leathers from the shop on Columbus, Iceberg shirts from Century 21, military surplus pieces with shoes meant for playing ball. On any given day a mash up of burgeoning actions sports labels or workwear staples mixed with traditional menswear pieces and finished with an inch-thick, solid gold herringbone chain for a wholly new take on menswear. With New York as his playground, with its big brand flagship stores and niche speciality boutiques all firing off together amidst cultural shifts and under the banner of the birth of hip hop, building a wardrobe became sport. I always like to remind people that when we were teens, there were very few people marketing to us.

There was no hoopla comparable to that of the baby Millennials. For sheer lack of power in numbers, no one was very interested in capturing our attention. So we invented new looks out of stuffy garb made for mom and dad mixed with vintage and the new things our contemporaries were making (shout out to the early pioneers of streetwear – you know who you are) like logo appropriation tees. Before streetwear collaborations became old hat, maybe before they were a glimmer in a marketing eye, my husband was trimming Stussy stickers, from the skate shop in SoHo where he worked, with an X-ACTO knife, carefully applying the double S link logo to the back heels of his Timberland boots. *Special edition. You can't get these. Very rare.* To this day, he folds his clothes and organizes his closet with a slow and deliberate reverence that I can only muster on some occasional Chinese ceremony. A baby blessing. A visit to ancestral graves. To say he takes his clothes seriously is an understatement. I fell in love with him way back when one of his mainstay wardrobe staples was a super heavy Versace belt bedecked with metal Medusa heads. We both felt sad when that thing finally fell apart from years of daily wear. On one of our first dates he wore a short-sleeved button-down shirt in royal blue with half-dollar-sized white polka dots. Polo. Maybe a shirt my dad would have worn in his very late life at the insistence of my sister and I that it was cute. But maybe not.

When Edina, Deirdre and I started our agency, BPMW, in 2003 and later our tradeshow (capsule) in 2007, we knew that the menswear landscape was changing: that somehow there were guys all over who liked looking good, whether in the quiet style of my dad or the wayout, pioneering style of my husband. I'd seen my dad get psyched over that storytelling at Banana. I'd been shopping with my husband and saw his passion for hunting and gathering rival even my own. And, yes, I liked it. It was, after all, much more attractive to me than my one ex-boyfriend who wore, without irony, a pair of green denim pants that he'd had since RISD graduation circa 1985 just because he didn't ever give clothes a second thought. That didn't

seem reasonable to me. Hell, I like a man with style. Who doesn't? So back just around the millennium, whether it was the ever-equalizing of the sexes, the great stuff happening in Japan on the tail end of the American streetwear scene in the 1990s, or just something in the air, my partners and I had a hunch that menswear was going to pop. In our (practically pre-gentrified) Meatpacking office building alone there was us, Thom Browne, Alexandre Plokhov with Cloak, all plotting away, cutting fabric and spinning PR stories. Collectively shaping and thinking about how men could and would want to dress in a way that was modern, masculine and relevant. There was *Cargo* magazine and the short-lived *Men's Vogue*, plus all those hybrid titty/lifestyle mags such as *Stuff*, *FHM*, *Maxim* and the like. Were men the new women? Well, they could never be that. Ahem. Anyway.

And then the internet exploded. And so too did menswear. Here were all these guys we'd been thinking about, who the young designers we were championing had been designing for. Following in the footsteps of the early birds who posted on the New York-centric Splay.com (lots of them making clothing too), here were guys, young and old, from all over the world, trolling in cyber chat rooms and whoa…they really cared. On Superfuture and Styleforum they were chatting about the blown-out crotches of APC denim, the quiet ease of a Steven Alan shirt, the latest Supreme release, and about Nike. Of course, Nike. Before e-commerce opened up sartorial trade channels, there were posters wanting to swap. *'Bathing Ape windbreaker from Nort. Size L. Doesn't fit me. So bummed.'* Provenance began to matter. Made in the USA. Even better, Made in Japan. Sneaker companies brought their freaky colourways to the US market and guys were falling over themselves for new releases. Big brands whose products and styles had been co-opted for years by the urban-dwelling style setters, the 'advanced' consumer, if you will, began speaking to this new menswear consumer. You didn't have to go to Sears anymore for your Red Wings. The secret was out. Damn fine utilitarian boots that last, don't break the bank and looked just right were just what young American males wanted. The love affair with tried and true and trad American brands hit a fever pitch three or four years ago. Maybe it was the rise of Brooklyn, the brand (it is bearded and it is plaid). Maybe it was a pure yet new-fangled American optimism brought on by Obama's Campaign for Hope. Maybe it was just the latest thing for guys to get into and feel good about. A modern hobby? After all, in this uber-connected age, in cities all over the world working at a breakneck pace, hobbies of yesteryear like fly fishing or duck hunting, camping or, hell, even tennis require so much out-of-reach effort and seem so novel. But cruising the internet and getting into clothes, well that's an easy thing, isn't it? A thing related to trading information and learning about new things, feeling and looking good that sits right with most any kind of guy. College kids started blogging and then got hired by menswear publications. A menswear paparazzi sprung up from the depths of the myriad 'news' outlets online and guys started taking pictures of each other's outfits (you can't make this stuff up). The scene at Pitti Uomo got catwalky. The whole cacophony made women's fashion weeks around the world seem…tired. Menswear, and all these guys with carefully crafted outfits and this unbridled enthusiasm for peacocking, stunting, flossing, and even fetishizing, felt fresh. There was a pure newness and excitement that hadn't yet been bought by corporations. There wasn't even really a name for it. And then the kids discovered the Brits, the swaggery old-guard Italians, the Japanese fanatics, the high-fashion slim or short lines by Heidi, Thom and Ricardo. And on and on we go.

So where are the rules of menswear now? And what are they? There is nothing I loathe more than spewing on about what makes something stylish versus timeless versus classic: I'm all for lawlessness. Making one's own rules. I love the unbridled enthusiasm and genuine good nature inherent in most members of the forward-thinking community of menswear makers right now. I feel lucky to work with such an amazing bunch of brands, designers, reps and marketers within our small but inspired world: characters who work with gusto, a little bit of humour and a lot of heart. But what with all this rapid sharing of information and fandom going on, the menswear arena runs the risk of being polluted with the overwhelming and overly excited adopting of trends and the quick release declaration that certain things are over. *Hello and goodbye workboots. Hello and goodbye Hawaiian shirts. Hi printed suits. Goodbye raw denim. Oh hello again…now I'd like you a little fuller in the leg.* Dare I say, it's the sticking to one's convictions, the not caring about trends, the knowing what you love about the same thing again and again or even the writing of one's own rules that has always made menswear seem more interesting to me than the ever-churning, overly dictatorial, advertising-driven but never really new feeling women's market. Come on, guys, don't actually become the new women where fashion is concerned. Soon the cut of your trousers will become a joke, like hemlines rising or falling with the economy. Take cues from old school guys and their funny standards, like Woody Allen in his dowdy thinking man's uniform or my late father, from fashion peacocks who throw up the middle finger to whatever the 'industry' is doing and find joy in the creativity of dressing, like industry bigs Nick Wooster, Daiki Suzuki, Mark McNairy – my husband too. Wear what you wear with purpose and pride. Don't think about it at all, or go nuts and embrace your sartorial hobby with the enthusiasm of an aspiring pro athlete. Whatever you do fellas, don't become trendbots – it negates the fun, sex appeal and realness from fashion. And, frankly, that's never a good look.

WOOD WOOD

\X/ood Wood, like many of their
Scandinavian counterparts, is hard to categorize.
Part of the burgeoning menswear movement in
northern Europe, Wood Wood has garnered
a following through simplistic staples, nods to high
fashion and a penchant for big graphics. To label
it as heritage, street or whatever else would
do a disservice to a brand that is multifaceted by
nature, drawing upon a host of influences for each
seasonal offering.

Since its inception in Copenhagen over a decade
ago, Wood Wood has been shaped by its founders
and visionaries T Karl-Oskar and Brian SS Jensen.
The brand, under their stewardship, has actively
avoided categorization in order to shift the focus
of the consumer on to the functionality and form
of their work, rather than the associated stereotypes
of a certain sub-genre. This anti-classification
ethos has allowed them to produce well-rounded
collections, featuring utilitarian elements alongside
garments rooted in sportswear, while avoiding
the staleness that can develop from thematic
confinement.

Opposite and overleaf: Autumn/Winter 2012/13.

KELLY COLE

The brand Kelly Cole is, as the name suggests, run by the somewhat infamous Kelly Cole who was in charge of the Lo-Fi Gallery in Hollywood in the first decade of the 2000s. Cole himself brings a vast amount of experience, knowledge and skill to the brand, and works with Sean Hornbeak, also a part of this unpretentious label. Famous for being the 'Denim Doctor', essentially the go-to place and person for all things denim-related, he also worked with denim companies such as J Brand and consequently played a major role in the global phenomenon known as LA Denim.

Kelly Cole, a brand and retail experience in Los Angeles, offers western and southern European finesse and understatement mixed with a classic Californian practicality in clothing that is hard to find these days. Daring might be the appropriate word to describe the brand, or simply visionary and truthful to their own design and production aesthetic.

Opposite and overleaf: Inaugural Collection, 2013.

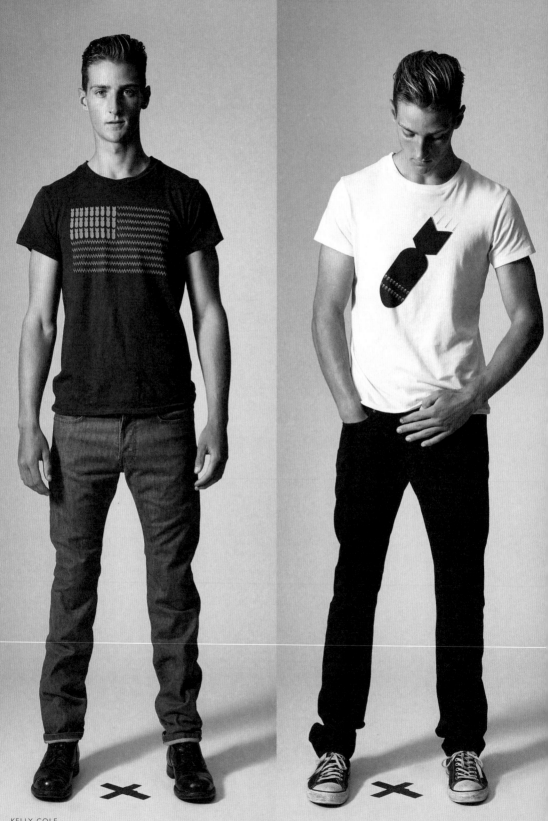

EAT DUST

A s with so many stories that read like an abridged version of a Brothers Grimm tale, Eat Dust was started by two close friends in Antwerp because they wanted to create their own brand. Unlike the gazillion other start-up clothing brands, though, both Rob Harmsen and Keith Hioco not only know exactly what they are doing, but also have decades of industry experience, a ton of integrity and the right kind of 'screw you' attitude. Harmsen has a very experienced sales background that reaches across several continents and all the major denim brands, as well as having an incredible eye for design, whereas Hioco comes from the birthplace of minimal cool, the Royal Academy of Fine Arts in Antwerp. He subsequently worked as a designer for a few big-shot denim brands, serving his tenure at RAF SIMONS before starting Eat Dust.

Heavily influenced by its involvement in the custom motorcycle, music and art scenes, the brand is breaking barriers and balls by simply putting out unexpected collections, as well as maintaining a staple line of denims with great integrity.

Preceding pages, right and opposite:
Campaign images by Michael Schmidt.

GOLDEN BEAR

amily-owned businesses are rare within fashion, as are brands that have lasted longer than 50 years. San Francisco sportswear brand Golden Bear is a rare exception. Their longevity feeds into their authenticity and is further complemented by the sheer quality of the product. Golden Bear specializes in classic American sportswear, providing a hard-wearing, ready-to-wear line that is largely comprised of work shirts, varsity and leather jackets. Golden Bear also provides a made-to-order service: a quaint but fantastic option in a world of fast fashion for faceless consumers.

Founded in 1922, Golden Bear initially catered for the city's dock workers, providing durable outerwear that served a practical purpose. Fast forward a couple of decades and the brand gained further notoriety by providing the pilot jackets of the Flying Tigers, Hellcats, P-38s and The Flying Fortress during the Second World War. Throughout the 1960s, stars from the burgeoning San Francisco music scene, and further afield, ventured to the city's Mission District in search of custom band jackets. From American presidents to the likes of The Grateful Dead and Jefferson Airplane, Golden Bear has been inconspicuous in its presence throughout various facets of American culture for the best part of a century.

Below: Golden Bear's HQ in San Francisco; opposite and overleaf: the brand's array of classic Americana-style outerwear.

18 WAITS

tarted in 2009, Canadian brand 18 Waits is coming close to creating an all-ncompassing zeitgeist rather than 'just' fashion. Granted, on the surface, the reinterpretation of well-versed classic menswear is just that, but dig a little deeper into 18 Waits and it becomes clear that there is a creative depth and romanticism that makes it a stand-out brand.

The somewhat superficial standard of quality and fit are all, seemingly, easily achieved with their clothing, but it is the entire presentation, the story and creation of their products that leads to the conclusion that what they do has a great deal of depth. Each collection since the inception of the brand has grown both in size and complexity. Despite the rugged and functional appearance of the clothing, it is incredibly detailed, made with great attention to detail and appreciation of the workmanship.

More than a clothing brand, 18 Waits is a three-dimensional and philosophical representation of an expertly crafted alternative reality.

Opposite and below: Canadian workwear;
overleaf: Autumn/Winter 2011/12.

BE POSITIVE

Having spent several years distributing and retailing, as well as nearly everything inbetween, Italian-based Slam Jam finally turned their hand to creating a footwear line in 2008. Be Positive sought to combine the elegance of classic Italian footwear with sportswear nuances. The allure of the brand derives from its versatility, eschewing stuffiness while creating products that are familiar and wearable.

In recent years, Be Positive has enjoyed a healthy collaborative relationship with Stussy Deluxe, among others. It is testament to those behind Slam Jam that they noticed the shifting trends and desires of consumers, many of whom began to shun sneakers due to their ubiquity but still desired the levels of comfort to which they had became accustomed after years of rocking runners or court shoes.

Right and opposite: Crafted Italian shoes; overleaf: the brand is an off-shoot of Slam Jam.

MAKING THE MENSWEAR COMMUNITY: POP-UP MARKETS ENTICE, ENGAGE AND ENLIVEN NEW CONSUMERS

by Nicholas Schonberger

Aside from being one of the co-authors of this book, Nick is an established writer, editor and curator for a number of print and online publications and even museums. His analytical insight into any subject is second to none in this industry, as are his wit and sarcasm.

How do men shop? That question, essential in an age of accentuated attempts to cultivate fresh clientele, defines how and where brands engage with potential consumers. The very idea that men indeed *do* shop requires a recalibration of retail. After generations of a status quo idea that men abhor shopping, a dirty little secret has been let out: in the right circumstances men care and want to invest time in bettering their wardrobes and even just talking about clothing.

Sounds familiar, right? The spectre of metrosexuality still remains: the notion that men care about their appearance remains from the time that confused word buzzed from urban media through the United States's vast malls. However, an essential difference in approach has emerged through the rise of 'menswear'. While the generation just before the digitization of style channels pushed fashion, the community that has risen thanks to open source platforms including Blogger, Tumblr and Wordpress celebrates a more nuanced sense of what men want and refocused attention on the fundamental values of upwardly mobile urban dwellers. The blossoming of 'menswear' owes much to online community building.

'The metrosexual movement's inherent foundation was based on the nefarious presumptive notion that it was inherently "gay" for heterosexual men to care about the way they look,' says Lawrence Schlossman, author of the tongue-in-cheek era-defining book, *Fuck Yeah #Menswear*. '*#Menswear*, on the other hand, empowered men – straight, gay or otherwise – to take ownership of their closets.'

In its initial stages, the menswear aesthetic was hardly progressive. Pioneering menswear bloggers sought not to shake up the United States's foundation, but instead the brave keyboard wielding men championed a contemporary vision of tradition. If Wallace Nutting and other champions of the Colonial Revival drew lessons from a centuries-past craftsmen culture, menswear bloggers looked to the post-war status quo for grounding. Hunting, fishing

and true prep are treated with equal reverence to the slick suits of the Madison Avenue ad men and the Rat Pack. Rebel stars James Dean and Steve McQueen gave readers reason to re-evaluate their own attire – the badass jackets and sunglasses worn by both men are still available today and, better still, are often made in the United States.

While the change had no clear didactic bend – shopping American is vaguely political, but it's no mobilizing force – the emergence of blogs provided solid footing for widespread adoption of fresh thought, or at least ideas that reinforced that it was OK to think about garments. Prior to this, online activity surrounding men's clothing was the realm of forums. These were pointed, but often exclusive. Blogs, in contrast, allowed more fluid, voice-led conversation that welcomed readers and fostered new comfort levels with the dialogue.

'The rise of the menswear community benefited greatly from a variety of online efforts that helped bring focus to products outside of the traditional editorial channels of print and periodicals. Like forums and message boards before them, blogs were a new platform for discovery and conversation around everything men's fashion and lifestyle,' says Jeff Carvalho, editor-in-chief of Selectism, a menswear blog founded in 2007. 'Our staff began seeing a demand from menswear consumers for more locally produced goods with true heritage. Our coverage at that time offered a strongly curated view of "heritage" and Made in the USA goods but also focused on locally produced goods in England, Japan, France and beyond.'

Understanding the assorted interests essential to most American men, Ohio-born and Manhattan-based publicist Michael Williams launched his blog, A Continuous Lean, in 2007. The site, with its singular voice, developed into a locus of trend. One by one, Williams uncovered and highlighted a small American business rich with history. He prompted, in part, the fervour for heritage – a term employed at first to identify the authenticity of a brand, and later used as a marker of a particular look. On a cliff of financial ruin, American men looked back in time to find what they wanted. Then, slowly rabid readership proved something editorials about the new metrosexual hadn't: men care about things that have a story.

Williams's blog spawned other personality-led imitators. And those imitators, in turn, inspired others. Soon a small population of male internet users was talking about something unimaginable, clothing. It was entirely new: A Continuous Lean and its ilk; discussion was out in the open and readily consumed by a diverse demographic. From the blogs emerged a tangible community. These outlets led to a community of people with shared tastes and values that has shaped and reimagined both the retail landscape and how men dress. Important to that growth is the transfer of conversation from online to physical space. Bloggers, not buzzword wielding marketers, were voicing the realities of the shopping man. And, in proactive stance, they also took charge in shaping an ideal commercial environment.

Like many good things, the Pop Up Flea started at a bar. Williams and his partner Randy Goldberg shared a thought: what would their ideal store look like? 'We wanted to open a store and we realized we didn't have the time or the crazy in us at that moment to open something permanent,' says Goldberg. Instead, they decided to produce an event and ultimately open their dream shop for one weekend and one weekend only. 'We thought it would be interesting to bring some of our friends together in one room, edit a selection of products and brands that we found interesting, and create a physical space for a mostly online community to gather and shop,' added Williams.

The ideas of the Pop Up Flea were congruent with emerging trends in bricks-and-mortar men's retail. Mickey Drexler, CEO of J. Crew, steered a once staid mall store back into the fray, and in so doing turned it into the very centre of the zeitgeist. Two things brought to life in Drexler's stewardship mark a significant change in men's retail: the J. Crew Liquor Store and the notion of 'in best

company'. Opened in August 2008, the Liquor Store occupies a small former bar in Manhattan's wealthy TriBeCa neighbourhood. Alongside J. Crew staples, the shop stocks classic garments – waxed jackets from English shooting favourite Barbour and American-made wingtips from Alden – asserting a trajectory of style and also camaraderie in quality. The store signalled the 'boutique-ification' of big retail and asserted the notion that a great wardrobe is built on a foundation of perfect individual pieces. However, something was missing. Despite superb selection, consistent with blog-world staples, the Liquor Store didn't quite satisfy a need for 'IRL' (in real life) interaction. With that unfulfilled, Goldberg and Williams had a niche.

Both Goldberg and Williams love flea markets. They ran with that classic set up, giving it an upscale feel and a menswear focus. A wide-ranging bunch attended – the first Pop Up opened in 2009 – representing hardcore online fans and casual passersby alike. All were treated to direct-from-brand sale, and an opportunity to chat with the proprietors of each, one on one. If the J. Crew Liquor Store proved that the men behind the menswear scenes could change retail, the Pop Up Flea exposed the inner workings of the industry to a real audience and encouraged a unique trust between seller and buyer.

'The community in contemporary menswear is a rather close-knit group with a lot of camaraderie, generally speaking. Within the finer segments of market/product divisions, e.g., high fashion vs. traditional clothiers, there are worlds of difference. Not just in markets, but in the importance of look over provenance, etc.,' says Gitman Vintage's Chris Olberding, one of Pop Up Flea's original vendors. 'Nonetheless, the underlying link that holds it all together is the growing awareness of a thing called "menswear" outside of the community by the consumer – call it the positive thread that weaves us together.'

The event bridged a gap. On one level, the Pop Up Flea is a sort of neo-tradeshow: brands highlight their best wares, consumers buy. The small-scale of the Flea allows for one-off and special edition products, all the more enticing to visitors. Beyond this, the Flea functions as a decommercialized hangout. Many attendees simply come to see their favourite brands, and the people behind them, in the flesh. Label owners, free from the stresses of wholesale, also have greater opportunity to chat among themselves.

'This was one of the nice moments for us at the first Pop Up Flea. We would hear vendors talking to other vendors about factories, about how they make things, about design from past seasons, and there became this great community aspect to the event,' says Goldberg. 'People have gotten jobs, brands have started collaborations, and ideas have been spread on how to make better things, all from interesting people being in the same room together at the Pop Up Flea.'

In short, the Pop Up Flea presented a palpable sense of community. Its success, like that of A Continuous Lean, created a lane for similar assemblies around the world. Also founded in 2009 and managed by the Pierrepont Hicks brand, Northern Grade expanded from its native Minneapolis to include pop-up markets in Chicago, Los Angeles, Nashville and Seattle. In Vancouver, Free/Man presented two iterations of Gentleman's Reserve, the final in 2012. Goldberg and Williams expanded their stake in 2013, bringing the Pop Up Flea to London…coincidentally staged just as J. Crew was opening its first UK flagship on Regent Street in London.

Consideration of pop-up markets opens up a lane to assess the core connective thread in contemporary menswear. Fashion, style and trend have a role. However, the real lasting legacy of the era is the connection of clothing to universal lifestyle. In an increasingly digital world, menswear offers a place of lo-fi reflection. The privileged silhouettes are a reminder of simpler times – camping or fishing, or when hand labour outweighed keyboard-tapping office gigs.

People have looked back before. As skyscrapers towered rabidly in expanding cities, the American pastoral calmed fears. Menswear's ideals even have precedent in the nostalgia boom that followed

9/11 – a period when stylistically Americans sought immediately comforting memories from sport or popular culture. Expressive of both acceptance of digital integration into daily life and a reverence for human production, the menswear community balanced the fast pace of contemporary life and proved the potential to slow down.

This truth is best articulated in the pop-up markets. Spurred online and realized in actual life, the markets opened opportunities for progress and amplification of ideals. Empowering consumers and connecting them to brands minimized a formerly impenetrable gap, fluidly engaging new voices in a conversation that had once been relegated to a small group within the industry.

As such, more and more small brands are arriving on the scene for a reason no greater than the truth that, by god, people want this stuff. Men are aware. They care. Ultimately, men also enjoy and relish tidbits about sourcing and fabrication.

Many of the small brands represented in this book are those that helped solidify the market by agreeing to test the potential of the Pop Up Flea, Northern Grade and all their peers. Divorced of an overtly competitive spirit, the people behind the brands – like the people organizing events and buying the stuff – understood the power of creating tangible spaces of interaction. The communal spirit, the sharing of information and the overarching transparency give concrete specification to shared values which define menswear in this moment. Far bigger than a look, contemporary menswear succeeds through a distinct way of looking at the world that spans socio-economic lines and simply celebrates the merit of well-made, smartly produced garments. By way of blogs, pop-up markets covered the breadth of audience ready and willing to adhere to and spread forth the benefit of traditional manufacture and the economic worth in investing in local or small-batch goods. Cutting out the middleman, so to speak, introduced a new paradigm in which consumer, editorial and manufacture voice together dictate what is championed and elevate the standards of the overall marketplace.

CLOSED

losed was originally from Italy, where in 1978 the brand started from humble beginnings, fusing a smart, yet modern approach to unisex fashion. Today, the brand is operated out of Germany, where it continues its timeless production of high-quality garments for both men and women. Closed has always perfectly bridged the gap between playing with the incredible quality of materials found in Italy and injecting its own aesthetic sensibility into the clothing they make. Part Scandinavian, part Italian, its timeless clothing – and men's line in particular – speaks to an unassuming but assured consumer who is not often found. Add a serious number of mono stores, all of which speak a clear, minimalistic, yet tasteful, sober language, and Closed has over the past decades positioned itself as the quiet leader in its field in Europe and is now poised to do the same further afield.

Opposite: Germany's foremost menswear brand; overleaf: classic styles with minimalist detailing.

COMMON
PEOPLE

There comes a point for most designers when the desire to control their output truly comes to the fore and they take the daunting plunge into the unknown.

Starting a brand not only requires a vast amount of experience and investment, but also a degree of self-confidence that not everyone possesses. This was the scenario faced by Scottish-born Kestin Hare who, after having worked as the head designer at Nigel Cabourn for just under four years, sought to carve his own sartorial path.

Common People was founded as a brand that eschewed gratuitous design and avant-garde styling in favour of solid, well-constructed clothing. The vast array of vintage clothing that Hare was exposed to at Cabourn, where the collection numbers in the thousands, certainly informed the brand's no-nonsense aesthetic that draws heavily from traditional military wear. Such appreciation

of past styles was a hallmark of Hare's work even when he was a fashion student in Newcastle. He often unpicked vintage Dior jackets so that he could copy the patterns, before adding his own twist to them. The same principle still applies with Common People: it is something familiar but with a contemporary cut and a consideration of detailing and fabrics that elevate the garment.

Despite still being relatively new on the scene, Common People has already garnered a following, with consumers appreciating the quality and considered nature of the garments.

NAKED &
FAMOUS DENIM

aked & Famous Denim, despite being a raw denim brand among hundreds of others, is pretty unusual. It is also borderline crazy, but a nonchalant, care-free attitude distinguishes it from its peers. Not many brands would respond to Justin Bieber's request for free jeans to wear on tour with a link to where he could buy them. Perhaps it caused their banker a bit of anguish, but it is moves like this that form the foundations of a brand which seems to have genuine relevance and longevity.

Founded by Montreal-native Brandon Svarc in 2008, Naked & Famous sought simply to make great quality raw jeans. The idea was simple, at least at first look: gimmick-free, untreated denim that would stand on its own due to quality and fit, not celebrity endorsements. This ideal was even incorporated into the brand's name, aimed at satirizing the celebrity culture that many brands feed off to survive.

This anti-marketing stance is not only refreshing, but the money saved on marketing is instead invested in doing some cool and pretty crazy things, such as glow-in-the-dark or scratch-and-sniff denim. Each idea for these special projects inevitably sparks a degree of consumer interest, while allowing the brand to focus on crafting great fitting jeans from imported Japanese denim in its Canadian factory.

A spate of raw denim brands has sprung up in recent years. Even the likes of Uniqlo and Marks & Spencer have produced selvedge denim. Naked & Famous, however, continues to push the envelope in terms of what a denim brand can achieve.

Left: the brand's Canadian factory; overleaf: advert-free denim.

GILDED AGE

A few years before the internet and subsequently the rest of the world started getting more than mildly interested in beard oils and cravats, an independent denim company based in New York made a few waves – it was noteworthy because it didn't involve the usual insincere marketing spiel, Gilded Age simply produced awe-inspiring, high-quality denims. These days when even your worst-nightmare-come-true child labour factory in Bangladesh markets itself as an artisanal company, it is unlikely to make an impact, but in 2005 this was a new thing. Over the following years, Gilded Age continued to bring out collection after collection of quality denim, which in retrospect seems like an early example of what was to come in 'menswear' – small runs of high-quality products. Focused and always on point, Gilded Age has remained at the top of its field, especially when it comes to making some of the best jeans on the market.

Above and overleaf: Examples from the New York-based denim brand, also available in plain indigo.

WINGS +

Wings & Horns encapsulated
the essence of menswear before the word had taken
on its current connotations within the lexicon of
clothing obsessives. Some would even be inclined to
prefix that 'menswear' with a hashtag, but it is fair to
say that Wings + Horns has provided contemporary
menswear since its conception in 2004. The brand
seamlessly combines elements of workwear and
sportswear, in a style that has certainly gained
prominence in recent years.

Initially named Spruce, the company's early
forays into clothing were predominantly with
knitwear before it was renamed and branched
out. The brand's aesthetic was, and still is, heavily
influenced by the seven years that its CEO spent in
Japan. Quality construction and attention to detail,
which are hallmarks of Japanese clothing, also lie
at the heart of Wings + Horns. For all its Japanese
nuances, the brand remains proud of its Canadian
heritage, operating out of Vancouver.

Right: Spring/Summer 2013; overleaf: Autumn/Winter 2012/13.

HORNS

IS IT ONCE AGAIN TIME TO RE-IMAGE THE PLATFORM OF COMMUNICATION TO THE YOUTH MASSES OF TODAY?

by Jeff Carvalho

WWW.SELECTISM.COM

Jeff Carvalho is one of the founding members and editor-in-charge of Selectism/Titel Media based in Berlin and New York. Selectism has played a large role in defining and shaping the course of the contemporary menswear industry through its excellent and timely coverage of the market and trends.

1

n 1999 various online blog formats emerged, including the incredibly popular livejournal.com and blogger.com. Over the next six years the platform, originally developed for personal journalling, became a tool that would help fuel a new stream of journalism and storytelling, better known today as a 'blog'. Using a chronological approach to storytelling, the blog site and format opened the door for just about anyone to explore their interests, using tool sets that made it incredibly easy to publish and promote stories and ideas. From sites about the feel of knobs on vintage audio hardware to sites looking specifically at old Apple Macintosh hardware, the conversation in the latter half of the 2000s was found on blogs.

But blogs were not limited to just technology: in the world of sneaker wear and fashion, a whole new space was emerging that took the lifestyle culture beyond the forum and bulletin board platforms of conversation into the new blogosphere that would launch a variety of high-profile sites dedicated to this world and the lifestyle surrounding it.

As the likes of Gizmodo and Engadget battled and worked hard to be first to the street with product announcements and imagery around the latest new gadget, sites within the realm of sneaker culture and later fashion were swelling with content that kept readers returning for more. Sites such as Fatlace, Flytip, Slam X Hype, Hypebeast and Highsnobiety (a site owned by Titel Media, a company of which I am a partner) were no different in the quest to be first and were the first point of entry into a world of sneaker culture, products that revolved around lifestyle, many of them purely aspirational.

What was most interesting during these early years was how little the big corporations producing many of the products we covered paid attention to the emerging blog platform – many considered blogs to be detrimental to their businesses when discussing new products and delivery dates. While many brands largely ignored our requests for information during those years, they certainly paid attention when their intellectual property landed on blog sites and quickly spread across other sites into the day-to-day conversation of our readers. For a long time, brands would send cease-and-desist notices for takedown of the latest new collaboration shoe or product, but by then the story and more likely the image had spread exponentially across the internet.

For many brands, blog sites were seen as a stream that was difficult to avoid and even more difficult to disregard. Fans of the culture were asking each other which blog sites others were reading to find the latest and greatest in product – and brands were listening.

Unlike the record industry, which did its best to kill off sharing platforms that were delivering music for free, with no policing or control, the big players in sportswear eventually decided it was best to embrace the blog sites and the voracious appetites of their audiences. Nike and Adidas, to name two, understood sooner than most that they needed to embrace the conversations happening on blogs. Rather than continuing to send takedown notices of early looks at a new Nike Jordan, brands began adding the blogging platform to their marketing strategies, understanding full well that the platform would continue to move forward at an even more rapid rate. The smart brands also understood that a new form of content creation and, more importantly, new media impressions were being developed that could measure reach, demographic information and, later on, engagement; the data sets and data collection available would become mind blowing. The flat metrics of magazine sales and radio plays would pale in comparison to the data collection allowed by blogs and countless other platforms on the internet.

Brands understood that to control their intellectual property online required control of the conversation as well, and the only way to do this was to work directly with the blog sites in ensuring

the messaging was proper. Choosing which blog outlets to work with was a fairly easy decision back in those early days: you simply asked for traffic numbers. High traffic (and large readerships) granted a handful of blog sites the exclusive content they needed to continue feeding their audience. Exclusives brought friendly competition among the big sites and even faster delivery of news content to readers. Audience numbers rose and content rose.

Some, for a time, believed that blog sites (and the internet in general) would lead to a decline in print and magazine sales: the new Millennial Generation, born in the internet age, was raised with a screen in their hand, not a newspaper. They certainly did not help the cause.

The blog format was successful and many, many others joined the explosion and conversation.

Towards the end of 2007, a decision at Highsnobiety was made to service an emerging reader who was coming online looking for men's fashion (menswear); a reader not too dissimilar from the sneaker and toy collectors who made Highsnobiety what it was.

This consumer was looking for quality goods over the need for printed t-shirts and disposable fashion. They were also interested in reaching back to a time in menswear when quality and production played an important role in American manufacturing. They wanted more than what was in the pages of *GQ* and *Esquire*, and hoped that by looking online they would discover new and

IS IT ONCE AGAIN TIME TO RE-IMAGE THE PLATFORM OF COMMUNICATION TO THE YOUTH MASSES OF TODAY?

124 → 125

undiscovered gems in men's fashion. For us at Highsnobiety, the timing could not have been better and we hoped to take the formula and the curatorial eye found on that very site and apply it to this new emerging menswear reader with the launch of Selectism.

As blogging platforms allowed Highsnobiety to thrive in 2005, the same platform shift in menswear in late 2007 allowed for Selectism to hit a reader that very few were talking to. The menswear market was just beginning to grow online and blogs like ours were there to service them.

More and more brands began to understand the value of the platforms built by a handful of individuals, many new to the journalism game. Posts and photos placed on sites such as Selectism and Highsnobiety would help sell inventories of products and goods for the brands and shops selling their wares through online and offline channels. Trade shows would emerge that catered to retailers who themselves catered to the online reader: many shops launched blogs of their own to help keep the shopper and conversation on their sites.

But like old media or print and magazines before blogs, new platforms would emerge at the latter end of the 2000s that would begin to shift the conversation – if ever so slightly – to a new place: the phone screen. Platforms such as Facebook, Twitter and, most importantly, Instagram began to attract users into spaces that allowed readers and not the content creators to control the conversation.

Engagement, that difficult to describe and yet easy to measure interaction between any content and a reader, became the hallmark in measuring a brand's success and reach. These tools would light a fire under the blog sites who quickly understood that a conversation shift was happening. The smart ones quickly embraced new platforms and their ever-growing audiences as tools to complement their sites. Those that did not were simply hampering their own growth in the new age of platform.

I often receive emails from young writers and bloggers asking for tips and advice on how to expose their blogs in today's world. I tend to respond with a flippant 'don't bother', but not without explaining to them that the platform and conversation has moved. Rather than focus on starting a site, I tell them to look to the new platforms for help in exposing their point of view to the audience at large. While the readerships on Highsnobiety and Selectism remain strong, today's world has moved to Facebook, Instagram and Twitter (in no particular order). They would do best to embrace these platforms and others such as Google+ sooner rather than later or the conversation will pass them by.

WON HUNDRED

Fashion seems to revolve around periodical hubs. For years, high fashion was largely the domain of Paris, only for a generation of six designers to emerge from Antwerp and take the industry by storm. This, in turn, shifted the focus somewhat away from the French capital. Similar hubs of creativity are dotted throughout fashion and tend to define periods worth remembering. The emergence of the Harajuku scene in the 1990s, and with it now legendary names such as Hiroshi Fujiwara, Nigo and Shinsuke Takizawa, redefined not only streetwear but also consequently menswear. Nowadays, every high fashion designer wants to reappropriate that street edge for their runway collection. Perhaps in the future we will look back upon the current Scandinavian crop of menswear brands with the same fondness that old streetwear heads do when they reminisce about the days of BAPE and Goodenough. While it may be too early to determine the lasting effects of the clean, stripped back Scandinavian look that has become most prominent in recent years, it is undeniable that this movement has provided a fresh perspective on menswear. Often fusing together elements of Americana with more fitted European silhouettes and the odd street-inspired graphic, brands such as

Norse Projects, Wood Wood and Our Legacy
have been the flag-bearers for European
menswear for the past five years. Among the
throng of prestigious Nordic menswear brands
rightfully sits Copenhagen's Won Hundred. As
one of the leaders of this so-called movement, it
has pushed this pared-back, clean-cut aesthetic
with considerable might since its inception in 2005.

The brainchild of Nikolaj Nielsen, Won
Hundred was born from a desire to challenge
the sartorial status quo in Denmark. Having left
school at 16 to pursue a career in fashion, Nielsen
spent several years learning the ins and outs of
the business before making the break to create
something he could truly call his own. It would
be fair to say that Won Hundred exhibits the
more grown-up end of the current Scandinavian
menswear movement, a movement whose popularity
Nielsen has in the past attributed to particular
Danish sensibilities. Speaking to Hypebeast in
2011, Nielsen mused, 'Danish designers have a way
of not taking themselves too seriously. Maybe it's
the *jante-lov*, which means you're not better than
other people. So we create cool things but we don't
make a big fuss about it. I think people like that!
It also comes down to personality.'

With Nielsen's knowledge from his time at Diesel and Sixty Group, Won Hundred initially started as a denim brand, but soon encompassed all aspects of menswear. Classic silhouettes are reinterpreted from a contemporary stand point, resulting in an array of simplistic and well-fitting casual and formal wear. Despite its relatively short existence, Won Hundred has grown and diversified as a brand, opening several shops across Denmark and branching out into womenswear.

Tobias Harboe, the menswear director, joined the company in 2011. Charged with designing four main collections per year, as well as the basic WH100 collection, Harboe drew upon his previous work with the renowned and eccentric designer Henrik Vibskov to execute classic styles with unique detailing. Often simplicity is the hardest thing to accomplish with a menswear collection because there is a constant temptation to tweak or add frivolous nuances. Yet, Won Hundred has consistently maintained its minimalist aesthetic without becoming stale. There is a lot to be said for doing the basics well. With a design process that limits flamboyancy, Won Hundred has allowed the quality of its garments to shine through.

Preceding pages, opposite and right: Autumn/Winter 2013/14; overleaf: Spring/Summer 2014.

HOWLIN' BY MORRISON

As a Scot myself, Howlin' always struck me as an incredibly odd name for a brand. As the Antwerp-based knitwear designers put it, the word is Scottish slang for 'smelly'. I have no idea why that seemed like a unique selling point to them. To me, the word has always carried connotations of something bad or generally distasteful, be it food, a certain smell or a pair of particularly ugly trainers. Despite this, Howlin' is anything but distasteful. Indeed, the brand's Scottish-made knitwear is generally fantastic and most likely smells just fine.

Howlin', formed in 2009, is a sub-brand of Antwerp's Morrison, which has been producing knitwear in Scottish and Irish mills since 1981. The brand provides a collection with real depth, considering it almost exclusively consists of knitwear, balancing accessories with chunky cardigans and stylish V-necks. The varied and often quirky hues complement the familiar styles that can be found in the brand's comprehensive knitwear offering.

Right: Autumn/Winter 2012/13; overleaf: various items of Scottish-crafted knitwear.

There are few menswear brands that can rival Grenson in terms of heritage. Founded in 1866, initially under the name William Green & Son before being shortened to its current incarnation some years later, Grenson has became synonymous with 'Goodyear Welted' English shoes. Today, Grenson continues to produce shoes using the same Goodyear technique that was championed in England in the 1800s, and it still yields fantastically durable footwear.

The classic English aesthetic of Grenson is understandable. A shoemaker by trade, William Green first learned his craft from his mother in her cottage. At the time, shoes were

GRENSON

still made primarily by craftsmen and women in small cottages. Green died at the turn of the twentieth century, leaving behind a factory of specialized shoemakers, but the brand continued to grow and flourish. Like many others, Grenson encountered great difficulties as a result of the depression in the 1930s, but in the 1940s the company was called into action to provide boots for British troops, which entirely revitalized the business. Somewhat ironically, the economic turbulence of recent years has done little damage to Grenson as the market for well-made, timeless shoes has grown ten-fold.

Left: Goodyear-welted English shoes; overleaf: Made in Northamptonshire, England.

GRENSON
138 → 139

STUSSY DELUXE

tussy, as a brand, requires little introduction. The brand's influence stretches far beyond clothes and, in fact, there are few facets of youth culture that haven't been affected in some way by founder Shawn Stussy's brainchild. To this day, Stussy remains iconic and, with its growth, has developed sub-sections akin to other brands of such stature.

Stussy Deluxe is pretty much true to its name, providing a product rooted in the Stussy aesthetic, but with higher thread counts and triple stitching.

Stussy Deluxe is rooted in American basics – seamlessly fusing the core brand's streetwear sensibilities with more refined cuts and considered construction. Such refinement is also translated through a more subtle approach to branding and graphics.

While many of us grew up with Stussy and its bold graphics, the Deluxe line provides minimalist garments with the same essence that first gave the brand its widespread appeal.

Opposite: A refined iteration of the mainline brand; overleaf: Spring/Summer 2013.

LIGHTNING
BOLT

Lightning Bolt started off as a Hawaiian surf brand in 1971 when Gerry Lopez, world champion surfer of the Banzai Pipeline, and Jack Shipley, surfboard shaping guru of North Shore, got together. In the early days, Lightning Bolt was known truly to encompass the vibe on the North Shore, which was reflected in the products it brought out.

A few years ago, Lightning Bolt was reignited with the help of Hawaiian-born surf veteran Jonathan Paskowitz. Since then, it has relaunched itself globally and is one of the companies to have benefited most from the renewed interest in vintage surf brands. Perhaps most notably, these days, the air and mystery that surrounds the original inception of Lightning Bolt still rings true. Spend any longer than five minutes with Paskowitz and you have yourself yearning for those far away Hawaiian islands and the incredible surf that blesses that part of the Pacific. This authenticity is effortlessly mirrored in Lightning Bolt's clothing.

Surf-inspired wares, Spring/Summer 2014.

STREET STYLE PHOTOGRAPHY: A BATTLE OF WILL

by Nicholas Maggio

Nicholas Maggio is a professional photographer with some skill, actually quite a lot of skill, which is something of a rarity these days, despite the abundance of photographers. Maggio originally attracted attention because of his blog, A Time To Get, but it has now taken a backseat to his photography.

Street style photography is nothing new: we've all seen the documentary on 84-year-old Bill Cunningham pot-shooting New York socialites and celebrities for most of his life. But with the birth of the internet age, the genre has grown into a beast, fuelled by blogs and iPhone apps. As the world grows smaller through social media, style hungry fiends can't wait until Sunday's style section anymore: they expect tomorrow's trends yesterday. A shot taken on Tommy Ton's Nikon can be downloaded to a laptop and uploaded to a blog within minutes of the shutter being snapped.

This means the style blogger in Omaha can dissect, praise, critique, summarize and post Nick Wooster's outfit before he even takes a step down McNasty's runway. This may sound excessive to some, but to fashion-obsessed readers around the world it's not so much a luxury as a necessity rivalling that of air and water.

Forget being in the right place at the right time – luck and serendipity. That shot of the bearded, tattooed guy wearing the blaze-orange beanie, perfectly worn APC jeans, fresh out-the-box Jordan IIIs, vintage Rolex, brown leather driving gloves and

Pea coat with camouflage lining crossing the street was not a fluke – it was a well-timed, thoughtful and calculated effort. Street style photographers know the spots. They know where the coolest walk and the setters sit. They know where and when to be to get the beautiful afternoon light bouncing off the 32-floor apartment building onto the north-east corner of the street. They know who to watch and where to see them. This isn't a game of chance but a battle of will. And believe it or not, they hunt for you. They track, trap and shoot in order to provide a fashionable meal for your eyes to feast upon when you wake up to your RSS feed.

And don't for a second think that anyone can do this, that anyone can pick up a camera and stalk every pair of brogues shuffling down Prince. This is an art unto itself – a photographic style falling somewhere between photojournalism, fashion photography and military sniping. Oh, yeah, and you gotta know what's right, what labels are being talked about in forums and what colours are clashing to blog-praising specifications. With companies offering professional grade cameras for half the cost of a pair of Visvim mocs, almost everyone with an index finger can take a decent photo these days. So the concerted effort to stand out as the sidewalk's elite rests is the amalgamation of art and knowledge. And only a select few have enough of both to allow their shots to be ushered to the top of Tumblrs. Reblog, Reblog, Reblog! The war cry of every street style photographer heard echoing throughout the dot Tumblr dot coms.

Whether or not regular folk understand the technical aspect of photography on an f-stop and ISO level, they recognize creative uses of a camera's functionality even if they aren't aware of it. Because cameras are so user-friendly to the point of the user being nearly obsolete, a photographer's style has become a crucial part of the street style photo game. When you see William Yan's photo of that nonchalant gentleman crossing Grand, you may not notice the shallow depth of field and lens length, but rest assured it was not only meticulously thought about, but done so at a moment's notice. It's these subtle yet paramount elements of a photographer's style that set them apart.

Anyone can take a photo. But a good street style photographer, loaded with an arsenal of Tumblr education, magazine familiarity and technical know-how, gets the shot every time. Like a chef whipping up a lasagne from scratch in a stranger's kitchen, street photographers worth their salt work with what they have, when they can get it, to create something worth a 'like' or a 'reblog'.

You can blame them for the guys in St Louis looking as fresh as the gentlemen in Soho. You can point fingers at the street style photographers for the bloggers in Texas having as much clout as the magazine based in London. The internet made the world small, street style photographers helped to dress it better: plaid-clad war photojournalists documenting the battle of the best dressed; Leica-toting fashion photographers redefining the editorial; well-armed snipers picking off the blog's favourite bearded personalities. Contemporary street style photographers are defining a genre, documenting an age and bringing style to the masses, one click, one upload, one reblog at a time.

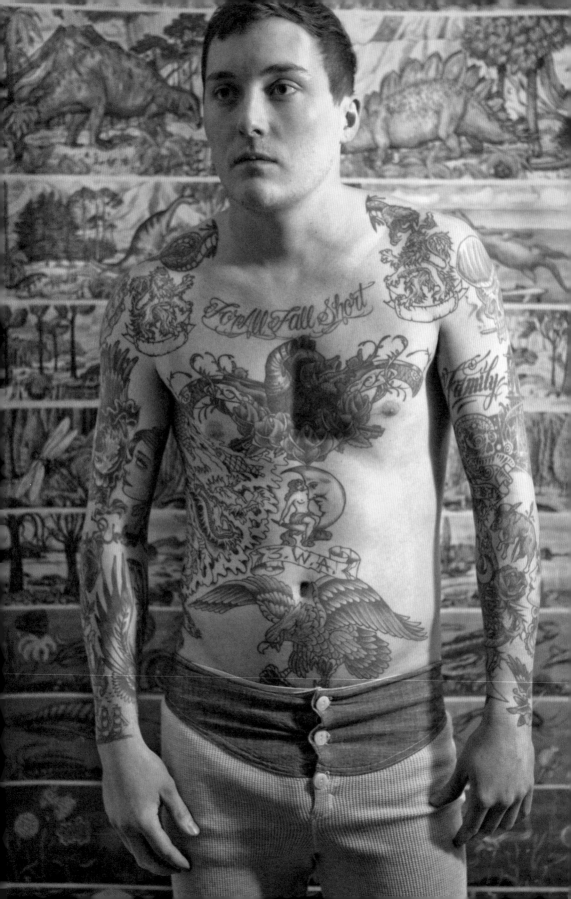

LEFT FIELD NYC

'I try to make pieces that are the best of class for a fair price' – Christian McCann is direct about his brand, Left Field NYC. The brand name is fitting as McCann began producing clothing in 1998 – at a time when hand-crafted staples were a truly out-of-the-box idea.

McCann's vision for Left Field blends an obsession for detail with a healthy, off-beat sense of humour. His vision of American clothing incorporates images of tough biker gangs and memories of AC/DC's Angus Young shredding the stage in fitted shorts. It's an awesome balance, one in which drawing influence from an Australian and producing American-made clothing makes complete and total sense. McCann's passion for finding and using off-kilter fabrics also gives each piece unmistakable personality. His take on classics is distinct, powerful and vivacious.

Based in Greenpoint, Brooklyn, McCann still has a firm hand in all of Left Field's activities. The brand has grown from operating in a shotgun apartment to maintaining a flagship store – located, in line with the brand's pioneering spirit, in Queens's up-and-coming Ridgewood.

Opposite: the undergarments range; above: the company is Brooklyn-based.

How did you start in clothing?

My girlfriend was working for Urban when I was in my twenties and she told me about this new store called Anthropologie. I was on my last month of unemployment so I went out and took a job. After a couple of months, I developed a relationship with the men's buyer (they did sell men's clothes some time ago) and I hustled my way into being an assistant, and then they fired the buyer before I started. So talk about sink or swim – I reported to the president of the company, now CEO of Urban, and somehow kept afloat for another couple of years until they shut it down, and I moved to Brooklyn where I started Left Field. While I was there, I discovered Kinokuniya and Japanese fashion mags and never turned back. I am inspired by old world craftsmanship, which is a dying breed, so mostly old

things. I walk Brooklyn Flea a lot, check out high-end vintage shops, antique stores and just wander around New York looking at architecture and freaks.

Why undergarments? And why differentiate those pieces with a different brand name, Choctaw Ridge?

It was the only piece missing from the perfect wardrobe – everything else was already there and it was kind of staring me in the eye, like do this now and make it like it used to be with that old world craftsmanship, with an eye for detail and fit. I wanted this to be a completely different vibe from Left Field, more turn-of-the-century dandy vibe. The name has nothing to do with underwear but has everything to do with Americana at its finest. It's derived from 1960s country singer Bobbie Gentry's 'Ode to Billie Joe'. It's a beautiful song.

Where do you draw the reference points for Choctaw Ridge from?

Well, the key inspiration was the old undergarment boxes from the 1940s, which have amazing graphics and are nice and sturdy. They're not like the make-it-yourself gift boxes you get nowadays that come flat packed and are all flimsy and crooked – they're solid, good quality garment boxes. The tags and stickers were really cool, too, with lots of bravado talk about their garments: kind of like old-school hip hop. There are some really cool garment details I have included as well and am continuing to add to the collection. The Choctaw Ridge hang tags are double-sided letter-pressed on antique German machines made in Ohio, as well as the boxes. We can still manufacture these things in America. Stop buying everything from China, people!

Are there any difficulties producing these garments in the United States?

I try to use the best factories at a competitive price, but it's very hard to make small-batch quality garments cheaply. Unfortunately, it's not easy to make quality items at low prices in New York due to the cost of real estate and wages. It's either bang-it-out sweat shops or high-end designer, with not much left in the middle.

Denim lookbook, 2012.

IRON & RESIN

Iron & Resin hails from one of the finest places in California. Nestled just off the beach in Ventura, the brand is infused with and seemingly born of those qualities that make Ventura such a great place. Unlike many of the other coastal towns in central and southern California, Ventura still retains a breath of honest, down-to-earth working-

class attitude, mixed with the ever sought-after hippie and surfer vibe that is now lost in most places out in the west.

These are some of the many reasons why Iron & Resin seems to ooze integrity and authenticity in a market mostly devoid of it – it is not trying to be anything other than what it is. Custom motorcycles, surfing and the vast expanses of California go hand in hand with the brand's clothing and accessories. Iron & Resin was started by a group of friends and industry veterans who took a fresh approach, which included a clarity in execution and the willingness not to compromise on the integrity of the brand. It is this ingrained authenticity, one that isn't even marketed, that makes Iron & Resin convincing.

Preceding pages, above, opposite and overleaf: Spring/Summer 2013.

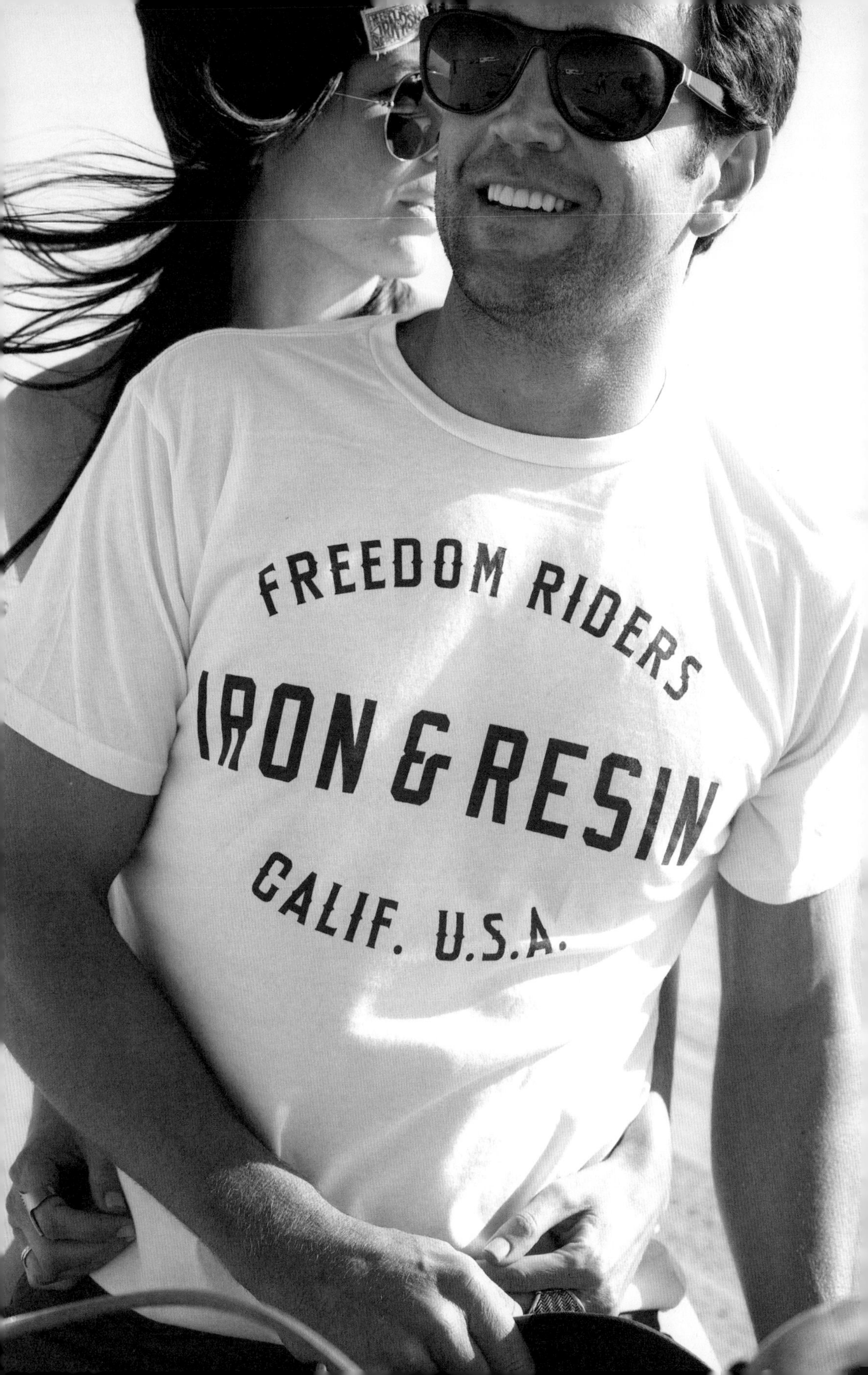
FREEDOM RIDERS
IRON & RESIN
CALIF. U.S.A.

PUBLISH BRAND

2011 was a shifting point in menswear. Once risk averse, designers were beginning to stray from traditional patterns and draw on some of the flair that had captivated streetwear buyers just a few years before the dawn of the recession. Call it a merger or simply a more fluid contemporary take on aesthetic interests – an attempt to reinvent the new man. Publish Brand made its tradeshow debut at PROJECT LV in February 2011, with the main attraction being unique trousers and a signature camouflage print. 'The camo was designed for the sense of "camaraderie", explains founder and

creative director Michael Huynh. The print is the link between the brand's desire to fuse military and jazz influences – 80% safe and 20% risk is the ideal mix – to create fresh takes on the expected. A cinch-cuff pant, the jogger, gave classic trousers menswear charm (think rolled cuffs). Styled with sneakers, the trouser encapsulated the Publish idea, a fresh twist on the traditional.

As the brand developed, the influence of music and its impact on the design process matured. Fabric blocking and pattern clash give the garments rhythm and personality. The pieces are bold, but coolly so…there's a subtlety to the hits that doesn't skew to ephemeral trends. 'We are very much into jazz…a very timeless and classic type of music,' Huynh says. 'We would like to see the pieces of design and garments we put out in rotation for years to come.' The notion of the jogger pant has certainly taken root. And, if Huynh's claim that 'once your "work" gets published, it's the crowning achievement of your lifetime' rings true, then the proliferation of similar trousers solidifies the idea that bridging menswear and streetwear captured the moment perfectly. The Publish brand mantra 'today for tomorrow' very much holds true in its design niche.

Preceding pages:
Spring/Summer
2013; opposite,
right and
overleaf: Spring/
Summer 2014.

TANNER GOODS

While much of Portland's sartorial shine is inevitably directed towards Beaverton, where Nike hold court at their colossal HQ, Tanner Goods have also put their name on the map in recent years. While knitted shoes and other such technical innovations are formulated and tested across town, Tanner look to the past, and the skill of knowledgeable craftsmen, in order to create their unique product. This small leather goods company has garnered a reputation for providing premium quality and products that age beautifully.

Each Tanner Goods product, be it a belt, wallet or bag, is fashioned from domestically sourced leather. They are assembled and sewn by a team of craftsmen, some of whom have been honing their skills since the 1960s. It is such dedication to quality and appreciation of the complex intricacies of their craft that has led to this small company being courted by several menswear brands for collaborative projects. Tanner's products are built not only to last, but also to improve with time and wear as, much like raw denim, they develop patina and characteristics unique to their owner.

Opposite: Autumn/ Winter 2012/13, timeless leather goods.

Above: Wilderness Rucksack; below: camera strap; opposite, above: Everyday Tote, key Lanyard and glasses case; opposite, below: Nomad Duffel.

AETHER

The words 'California Cool' conjure distinct images. For example, there's the Hard Edge style of mid-century painters and the clean lines of their architectural contemporaries. You might also think of Jeff Spicoli in chequerboard Vans. Of course, most of the world just envisages the classic American style of the laid-back surfer. All connotations are valid: the essential vibe of the place is an acute balance of beach, desert and mountain: Venice, Palm Springs and Bear.

When it comes to technical outerwear, California is no stranger to industry leading innovation. The state is home to the brand Patagonia and the spiritual origin of The North Face. Beyond, the state boasts roughly 840 miles of coastline and genuinely impressive mountains. In short, the Golden State is an outdoor lover's paradise.

Just as design and the outdoors collide naturally in Cali, so does a need to balance the city and nature. Aether, founded by Palmer West and Jonah Smith, connects those points through the sophisticated lines of the brand's outerwear. Giving form and function equal footing, Aether designs without superfluous embellishment, allowing for garments that happily walk mountain peaks and urban streets.

Stripped to the essentials, Aether is about making wearers comfortable in any terrain. The form-fitting Fall Line shell, built of three-layer four-way stretch fabric, stands out as the brand's keystone product. Technically, it is about offering the greatest flexibility and range of motion possible. Its seams are sealed and equipped with an exposed waterproof zipper that can withstand wind and water, meaning it could easily navigate a weekend bombing the ski slopes. The jacket is also slim cut and sleek, so on a treacherous morning run to your favourite coffee roaster, when a downpour could damage your swag, there is still a chance you might catch the barista's eye.

Respect for material is essential to the Aether DNA. Designs are understated and performance orientated, using the capabilities and characteristics

Opposite: Autumn/Winter 2013/14.

of the chosen fabrics as guides for crafting the most useful, attractive goods. Still looking for a link to classic California design? Consider the iconic Eames DCW chair. Elegant, lightweight, functional and full of aesthetic integrity, this piece sets a great precedent for material-influenced design.

Of course, West and Smith aren't boldly talking about carrying the Eames legacy; nor do they make much reference to California's design heritage. Yet, it is impossible to view their collections outside of this context – the Aether office is in a 1953 warehouse refurbished by architect David Thompson and fitted with solar panels – and there is an inherent link. It is design in the simplest sense, attempting to solve crucial problems (technical capabilities in city appropriate cuts) and improve daily life.

Branching out from jackets, Aether has matured. Stores in San Francisco and New York expand on the brand's distinct aesthetic and celebrate a broad range of easy-wearing garments, from knits to swimsuits. West and Smith, slowly but surely, have absorbed the influences of their California home and recast the conception of the state back east.

Aether is cool. It is California. And it is unmistakably contemporary.

Above and opposite: the New York store.

VIRTUAL REALITY: HOW BLOGS ABOUT CLOTHES CHANGED THE RULES OF MENSWEAR

by Jian DeLeon

Jian DeLeon is a menswear writer from Virginia. Married to the 'blog life', he has contributed wit and wisdom to the pages of *Complex*, *GQ*, *Valet* and many other publications. He lives in Brooklyn, New York.

Before menswear blogs, online forums were the de facto safe space guys could freely discuss clothes. To any nerd, the bulletin board format was second nature; after all, the pre-internet thrived on communities based on primitive listservs and bulletin boards.

So it goes with menswear forums. Prior to Hypebeast's establishment in 2005, some of the more prominent were Styleforum, Ask Andy About Clothes and Superfuture. Ask Andy was the spot old men went to discuss American trad and tailored clothing. Designer Mark McNairy is infamous for being banned from there more than once. Styleforum catered to the same crowd, but eventually established a sub-board for fledgling denimheads and recovering streetwear addicts. Superfuture was the archetype for what #menswear would become: it was ostensibly about clothes, but it was more about community, and your membership due was your taste level. It was a place you could kick it, learn a couple of things about cool gear (especially all things raw denim) and maybe, if you spent enough time lurking, you'd learn a thing or two about cool clothes.

Of course, guys getting into clothes and caring about trends and labels isn't just directly due to these forums. Pop culture was also reinforcing the idea of the well-dressed man. Vampire Weekend showed that indie rockers could wear boat shoes and critter pants, while *Mad Men* ushered in a revival of 1960s style: slim, conservative suits, tie bars and well-coiffed hair. Meanwhile, an economic recession encouraged guys to grow out their beards, and instilled the notion that 'buying less, but buying better' when it came to clothing was a worthy investment. From this early Americana movement of the mid-2000s, men started thinking about style in a new way. Trendiness made way for timelessness, and the modern man wanted to look, well…a lot less modern. Whether a man wanted to emulate Don Draper, a disaffected prep or an urban lumberjack, guys who had no clue about

style now had an invaluable tool at their disposal: the internet.

'I still believe that a lot of dudes who started menswear blogs weren't on the forums. Either they didn't know they existed, or they felt like they didn't speak to them, so they went and created their own platforms for conversation,' says Lawrence Schlossman, editor-in-chief of tongue-in-cheek blog Four Pins and co-author of *Fuck Yeah Menswear*, a Tumblr-to-book that poked fun at a sub-culture that came to be known as '#menswear'.

Taking its name from the Tumblr platform that birthed it, the hashtag in #menswear refers to a tag that only a few select users were able to edit and deem content 'worthy' of being included in that tag, ensuring it got a wider audience. Schlossman was among the early adopters of the Tumblr platform and, as a result, his highly trafficked Tumblr How to Talk to Girls at Parties, named after a Neil Gaiman short story, went from a complement to his blogspot-hosted site, Sartorially Inclined, to an influential force in terms of documenting and commenting on what well-dressed men on the internet were wearing and what they should be wearing.

'The guys who are big on Tumblr now got to that point because they had already established Blogspots, Wordpresses or whatever. They had those Tumblrs as "inspiration boards" or supplements to their main blogs,' recounts Schlossman.

Indeed, such sites as You Have Broken the Internet, Unabashedly Prep and Street Etiquette had dedicated followings in their own right, and the Tumblrs they started originally were meant to promote the content they were posting on their 'main sites'. Before Tumblr's 'toy blog' platform proliferated, these content creators were still figuring out how to use it.

'If you wanted to present a point of view, it wasn't just a visual point of view. You had to write something. You had to *publish* stuff,' posits Sean Hotchkiss, a menswear writer who has had stints at *GQ* and J. Crew, and is currently the editorial director of SuitSupply.

2009 was a different online environment for men's style. Guys who were trying to find themselves sartorially had no qualms about documenting their journey online. They geeked out about perfectly fitting jackets and lookbooks, similar to the streetwear lames that hung out on sites such as Hypebeast and Selectism, but their earnestness came off as real instead of corny. What separated #menswear from forums and other forms of online discussion about men's style was that people got the sense that these were *real* dudes. They might have loved clothes, but they were passionate about it, and wanted to promote the benefits of being handsome.

Some of the early Tumblrs thrived on the image-heavy format. Sean Sullivan's The Impossible Cool gained popularity by offering up daily black-and-white photos of timelessly awesome gentlemen such as Paul Newman or Frank Sinatra. Stylist Roxana Altamirano's Nerd Boyfriend juxtaposed full-body shots of unintentionally well-dressed men such as Rick Moranis and Bill Murray with shopable items similar to their outfits. People were starting to figure out how to use the platform to say something new or to say old things in new ways.

Tumblr's – and #menswear's – prominence was acknowledged by the fashion industry when a select group of 'editors' was chosen to represent the platform at New York Fashion Week in 2011. Then fashion director Rich Tong marketed these young 'influencers' to brands and designers, boasting about the platform's popularity and obviously promising to give these brands shine in the form of endless reblogs. Famously, Tong's exorbitant rates for these services drew the ire of the industry. After all, what kind of self-respecting label wants to pay $100,000 for a couple of struggle posts from a teenage blogger? What did happen, though, was that Tumblr made street style mainstream.

'It definitely helped spread street style because it dissipates so easily. Tumblr is an amazing vessel from which to share images. All greater cultural impacts aside, it's just an easy way to share or find photos. Street style owes some of its proliferation to Tumblr; that's how shit spreads like a disease,' swears Schlossman, who was part of Tumblr's first group of New York Fashion Week bloggers. In addition to established guys such as Tommy Ton and Scott Schuman, a younger crop of street style photographers started popping up too.

Soon tradeshows and Bryant Park were full of people wandering around aimlessly with cameras: teenagers Liam Goslett and Noah Emrich went from being internet cool guys to paid photographers. Meanwhile, established industry figures with great style started becoming internet celebrities: most notably, Eugene Tong, Josh Peskowitz and Nick Wooster.

'Without Tumblr, we might not be talking about Nick Wooster like we talk about Nick Wooster. Nick would still have an important job in the fashion industry, but the idea of "Woost God" or Wooster as an icon wouldn't exist. The savvy voices of Tumblr helped create those personas,' claims Schlossman.

'Guys like Josh Peskowitz or Eugene Tong, you don't know how long they've been in the industry. All you see is this steezy dude and you're like, "well, I could be that dude. I'm a handsome guy. I can look like that!" But you forget that they've worked in magazines for like 10 years,' argues Hotchkiss.

Therein lies the problem with Tumblr and the rise of street style: it made dressing well a little more important than it should be.

'For some people it can be a hindrance to their job,' says Schlossman. 'No one wants to be just a pretty face or someone with a good wardrobe. These people's images got spread around enough that people wanted to identify them, and they became these sort of micro celebrities, not because they were trying to, but because Tumblr helped create the idea that being a well-dressed individual meant getting street styled enough.'

This 'idle worship' of these newly minted street style icons was one of the things that prompted Schlossman and Kevin Burrows to start Fuck Yeah Menswear. Its missives on the state of the industry and self-policing nature to the sub-culture it was partly responsible for were hilarious, but also signalled the apex of the whole #menswear thing. Of course, this level of meta-ness had happened in the streetwear world, too, as the mid-2000s had the short-lived Don't Believe the Hypebeast firing shots about pieces like Rogue Status's 'Gun Show' t-shirt (you know the one, it had guns printed all over it and every other person had one in 2007).

What many people credit Fuck Yeah Menswear with was bringing hip-hop lingo and rap references into the conversation about men's style. For some reason it worked well. Schlossman is an avid rap fan, so it was natural to him. On the Superfuture and Hypebeast forums of yore, kids had always talked this way. Just because their tastes were changing from 10.Deep to Thom Browne didn't mean their vernacular did. Hip hop was a form of realness and identity. Clothing and style, however, have malleable connotations.

'Kids' is the operative word. The most ironic thing about #menswear is that men weren't really the ones adopting its aesthetic and lingo, rather it was the Tumblr generation, which for the most part consisted of teenagers and guys in their early twenties.

'When people think of #menswear they associate it with a younger demographic,' posits Schlossman. 'If you think about the Americana movement, they were these older guys that were drawn to these super masculine things and I think that the #menswear generation is the idea of straight guys getting into fashion.'

If Americana guys got their style cues from the past, the #menswear dude had a more forward-looking view on clothes. He was a bit more open minded and well travelled, gleaning inspiration from the dapper grandpas of Italy in unstructured sportcoats and washed denim. It was a more global and distinctly European view on style, and the designers these guys championed reflected that.

Michael Bastian and Brunello Cucinelli were pretty much regarded as the highest standard of clothes. Other Italian brands such as Isaia and Boglioli suddenly developed a following among younger men. Aaron Levine of too-good-to-last brand Hickey revitalized Club Monaco's menswear.

Meanwhile, his old co-worker Ian Velardi launched his own line. J. Crew alumni Todd Snyder (the man behind the TriBeCa Liquor Store and the Ludlow Suit) struck out on his own too. Two Jewish brothers from Brooklyn decided to start a line called Ovadia & Sons after a chance meeting with Ralph Lauren in the Hamptons.

The post #menswear era is characterized by everyone being in on the joke, and men dressing so as not to be '*that guy*'. The irony came from the fact that these people who had learned so much about clothing and style from the internet now wanted to dress like they hadn't been dressed by it at all. This signalled a general shift away from dressing up all the time, and in terms of internet style culture, the guys who once championed double-breasted suits and double monk-strap shoes began to opt for Nike Free Runs and Unis trousers.

After the boom of #menswear on Tumblr, many of the voices and personalities who fully embraced and advocated it had found their way into the industry proper.

'When you get into the post era of anything, that's when the movement starts acknowledging itself. You saw that with Fuck Yeah Menswear and then blogs like Four Pins,' says Schlossman. 'You get the self-awareness, and you get this post #menswear landscape.'

Perhaps the 'jump the shark' moment was when Christopher Bastin chose to base GANT Rugger's Spring/Summer 2013 collection around a bunch of #menswear guys he dubbed #TeamAmericano. The team consisted of Lawrence Schlossman, Sean Hotchkiss, Noah Emrich, Gabe Alonso and Zeph Colombatto touring around Italy in the new collection.

M.Nii

The story of M.Nii began with one, or several, pairs of surfing trunks. As with many of the truly enchanting fables in surfing, this particular story also starts in Hawaii – specifically, on the island of Oahu in the mid-1950s. The spirit of these golden times of early modern surfing is often glorified and just as often misunderstood, but it is truly understood in this new inception of M.Nii. Originally, M.Nii was a small 'mom-and-pop' tailoring shop that catered for the growing surf scene on Oahu. But it quickly became a local legend because of the quality of its work and, more importantly, its signature surfing trunk. Over time this reputation grew globally, as did the appeal of surfing, and M.Nii became a badge of honour within the surfing community. The brand went into decline until recently when the idea, brand and spirit were resurrected by John Moore and his team at the Pencil on Paper (POP) Studio in Los Angeles. This was a stroke of luck for the name and ethos of M.Nii as Moore and his team are as ingrained in the concept of stoke and surfing as you could imagine.

Today, M.Nii is one of the finest independent surfing brands, reflecting the spirit of its fabled roots in its authentic collection of Made in the USA surfwear.

Opposite and above: the inspiration behind the brand's collection; overleaf: Made in the USA surfwear.

REIGNING CHAMP

K eigning Champ lives up to its name in the world of menswear. Based in Vancouver on the beautiful west coast of Canada, the brand is part of the larger CYC Design Corporation, which is known internationally for its unrivalled craftsmanship, ingenuity and adherence to quality.

Initially started as a core brand focusing on sweats, Reigning Champ has expanded to include tops, bottoms, outerwear and accessories, all made in the company's factory in Vancouver. At first glance the products may seem basic, but Reigning Champ deserves a special place in this book for its commitment to high-quality, well-fitting exercise clothes – no other brand shows such dedication to excellence in this niche. In addition to its excellent products, the brand has a marketing sensibility that speaks volumes about the people involved in the company. They have collaborated with Ace Hotels, Deus Ex Machina, Wings + Horns, DSPTCH, Takashi Kumagai and Beauty & Youth of United Arrows in Japan, to name a few.

Right, opposite and overleaf:
Autumn/Winter 2012/13.

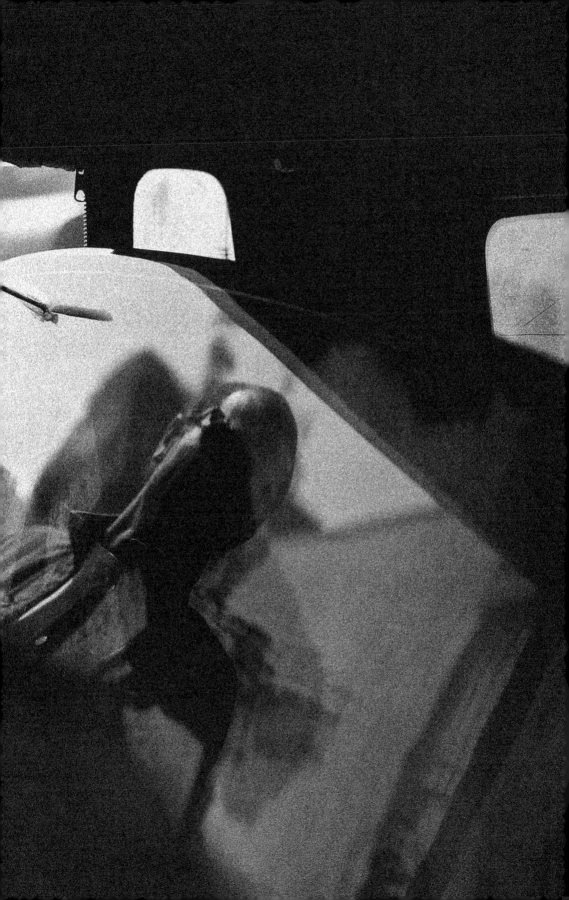

AITOR THROUP

In 2006, a phenomenon that had been bubbling under the surface announced himself to the sartorial world. Argentinian-born Aitor Throup came to the fore in his final year at London's Royal College of Art with his collection 'When Football Hooligans Become Hindu Gods'. 'There was a guy who sat beside me in classes who was a strict Hindu,' Throup explains. 'I learned through him and became fascinated by its symbolism. It also represented the transformation of me: in five years I'd gone from being surrounded by football casuals to sitting next to a Hindu at university.' The paradox between the working-class town of Burnley,

where Throup spent much of his youth, and the diverse cities of Manchester and London, where he formulated his creative outlook, is exhibited in his work. There are noticeable elements of his love of Massimo Osti, the visionary behind Stone Island and C.P. Company, in much of his work, but these are fused with deeply researched and creative narratives. It is this mixing of the analytical and the creative in Aitor Throup that has produced clothes that are genuinely different.

The press and the bloggers were not the only ones to take notice of his talent: 'When Football Hooligans Become Hindu Gods' also caught the

attention of well-respected menswear brands, in particular Stone Island. 'One of my tutors tipped off the guys who worked at Stone Island when I was in my final year. I was preparing for the three-minute catwalk show of "When Football Hooligans Become Hindu Gods" and something obviously sparked their interest enough to make

Preceding pages: Throup's Shiva Skull Bag (left) and design sketches (right); above, below and opposite: 20th anniversary C.P. Company Mille Miglia jacket.

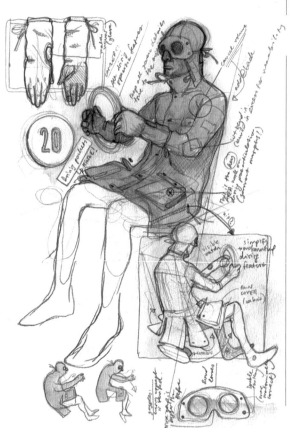

them get on a plane and come over from Italy.' The men tasked with assessing Throup's work were impressed by his ingenuity. 'Within a couple of months I was in Italy, I got to meet Carlo Rivetti [CEO and creative director at Stone Island] and we got on really well. I did two collections with them – that sort of proved myself to them. Then they asked me to do the C.P. Company 20th anniversary jacket.'

'When things become standardized,' reflects Throup in his London-based design studio, 'they are taken for granted.' In contrast, Throup spent much of his time at Manchester Metropolitan University questioning why such things were taken for granted. He did not want simply to create garments on existing blocks and 'decorate them': he sought to create something new that he could call his own, something that reflected his core design principles of reason and functionality. The result of this contrarian form of thought evolved into his ethos of 'branding through construction'. This ethos was formalized in a design manifesto published by Throup that outlines the thinking behind the way he designs his garments. Entitled 'New Object Research', the document curates his beliefs and ideas in an articulate breakdown of his creativity. 'It strikes a balance between being analytical and creative,' according to Throup. 'New Object Research', in the words of its visionary, is about 'designing processes rather than products. The designer creates a conceptual framework that is often informed by a narrative. The research dictates the specific physical processes. The designer then purely "curates" the product through strictly adhering to the process.' It is this conceptual side

of his work that allows Throup to straddle the worlds of product design and art.

The result of the 'New Object Research' process is clothing. Yet, it could also be construed as art, both in its construction and its exhibition. Throup does not adhere to traditional cycles of fashion in which a new line of clothing, with a different theme, is hauled out every six months. Such forced creativity does not seem natural to him. The depth that many of these collections lack is precisely what lends intrigue to Throup's clothing. Each concept is explored thoroughly, from New Orleans marching bands to Mongolian horsemen: nothing is left unexamined as ultimately it informs his whole process. This striving for correctness, as 'perfection', is not something he wishes to pursue. It has drawbacks, too. In 2010, Throup was due to present a collection from his 'New Object Research' line to a Parisian audience when unfortunately he had to pull the plug on the show at the last minute because the production from an Italian manufacturer was not up to standard. For Throup, it was simply a matter of integrity: both his own and that of his product. 'When I cancelled the Legs show in Paris it was a shame, but it also showed people that I had integrity and believed in only

doing things right. In hindsight, although it was a shame, it was the best thing that ever happened to me because it made me realize that we had to grow from within. It led to what we have today, where all garments are manufactured at our studio. It took us seven years of modifications to sewing machines to allow us to construct the garments in the way that we do.'

His output since he left the Royal College of Art in London has indeed been modest. The past few years have been about forming the building blocks upon which he can develop and prosper. His creation of archetypes that he can use for future collections has borne little fruit in a commercial sense. However, their development has provided the basis from which he can build future collections. It has allowed him to examine other areas of clothing design such as developing new fabrics in a similar manner to his idol, Massimo Osti, and improve his methods of in-house production in light of the Paris fiasco. Throup speaks of a hierarchy to his design process, 'all features are traceable back to the process, and therefore the concept and narrative', leaving colour as an afterthought for the time being. While he admits there's a good chance that future product releases will involve

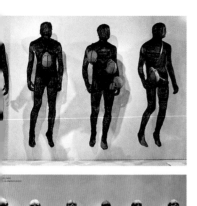

'New Object Research' installation.

colour, for now 'black sets a tone which allows you to focus on the garment and its construction.'

So far, Throup has managed to sell all his releases through progressive retailers such as Dover Street Market in New York and Oki Ni, who are unperturbed by the price tag and enthused by the freshness that his designs bring to the table. 'The retailers we work with have been very supportive,' says Throup with a humility that suggests he is genuinely appreciative of those who 'get' his work. Even after hours of research on his work prior to our interview, such an eschewal of the uniformities of fashion still seemed a relatively alien concept to me: I may be well versed in raglan and inset sleeves, but not this type of garment construction. Despite being captivated by his ideas, it was only after an hour of conversation with the man that I began to understand the conceptual basis for his work and its marriage with tangible form.

'I struggle to switch off from work,' laughs Throup, a man clearly besotted by his research and craft. His creative endeavours are not merely limited to clothes. He also works as creative director for the band Kasabian. There is little telling what the future holds for Throup, although it may be more apparent by the time you are holding this book. There are, however, many who have an inkling that this man has the ability to shift the focus of how we view menswear. There are brands that he admires that conform to what he views as 'the limitations of the fashion industry', but it is simply not the way he does things. Although he foresees the creation of archetypal pattern blocks as something which will eventually allow him to produce more seasonal collections, it will not be at the expense of his creativity. He is not a maverick, he is too analytical, but he is perhaps the man who will signal a re-evaluation of the fundamentals of male clothing. 'I'm not saying that all clothing should have a conceptual depth,' he says. 'I'm just saying that mine does. Imagine if the music industry did it that way. Imagine if they released all their new music every six months. Every six months the artist would have to develop a new concept. You'd have to listen to the new albums all at once and you're only allowed to buy it for six months. After that you have to buy the new album.' It is a refreshing approach to menswear and one which may just catch on.

GITMAN BROS.
VINTAGE

itman Brothers are widely considered to be one of the best US-based shirtmakers and the brand's Vintage division has successfully carved its niche in a menswear market that has rediscovered a long-lost love for timeless Americana and prep-inspired wardrobe staples.

Gitman Vintage is a laidback, trend-conscious offshoot of Gitman Brothers. The brand itself has been making shirts for over 70 years in Ashland, Pennsylvania. The Vintage line draws heavily from the brand's vast archive of vintage styles and fabrics and reinterprets them from a contemporary standpoint. Each model is rooted in a classic style, but is given a fresh lease of life through slimmer cuts and fabric selection, which can range from subtle Oxford cloth to slightly brasher, all-over prints.

Each shirt is meticulously crafted, taking the seamstresses more than 80 minutes as they work their way through the 50 steps involved in transforming a chambray or a twill into a button-down Gitman shirt.

Opposite and overleaf: Gitman's vast fabric selection; right: the ubiquitous button-down.

PIKE
BROTHERS

The Pike Brothers' story starts some time in 1930, when George and Joseph Pike opened a small and specialized tailoring shop on Portobello Road in London, which predominately dealt with workwear at the time. With the onset of the Second World War and the influx of American soldiers to London, the Pike Brothers started making uniforms for the American Forces. They were known for quality work that combined the craftsmanship of European tailoring and the necessity of sturdy, functional workwear of the time.

Today, Pike Brothers make clothing with the same approach as the Pikes did back in the 1930s and 1940s. Their collections are based on well-fitting, sturdy denims, shirts and jackets that speak of a time when clothing was meant to last longer than a few months and yet not look like a sack of potatoes.

Below, opposite and overleaf: Autumn/Winter 2011/12.

GLENN KITSON

> Glenn Kitson is possibly best known for his work with the publication *The Rig Out*, which he co-founded. Aside from his work with *The Rig Out*, he is also a respected and internationally renowned stylist and brand consultant.

From humble beginnings in Bolton in the north of England to the upper echelons of niche fashion, Glenn Kitson is frank both in and about his work. Perhaps it is symptomatic of his upbringing in the north of England, where quality clothing is admired, but rooted in working-class sensibilities and simplicity. Glenn's work in the 'industry' initially found him in the field of vintage sportswear, selling and sourcing it around Europe. While his continental excursions provided broad horizons, his study of fashion communications at university focused and refined his skills. His creativity is apparent in his work, yet he avoids the perennial tendency of fashion to create images and ideas to which people struggle to relate. His philosophy is that clothes should be presented in a manner in which the genuinely wearable look is highly commendable in a vacuum of pseudo avant-garde creations. We sat down with Kitson to discuss menswear, but not too seriously, of course.

For those who don't know, what do you do?
I'm the editor and co-founder of *The Rig Out* magazine, a lifestyle publication that also lives online at therigout.com. As well as this, I consult for a number of brands and agencies (primarily menswear and sportswear) on all matters from art direction to marketing and strategy.

Now that we've nailed down your credentials, let's talk menswear: British menswear to be precise. For a small country, Britain's influence on the way men dress throughout the world is quite astounding. We're quite lucky in that respect, aren't we?
Every morning I wake up and count my blessings. Then I fall to my knees and praise Jesus.

What was it that first got you into clothing?
I know it's a cliché, but not having much as a kid and seeing what I didn't have. It's quite a working-class thing: clothes can elevate you out of your situation.

Football and music seem to be the seminal influences not only on British youth culture, but also on the way we all once dressed. Would it be fair to say that has been lost in present-day Britain?
No, I disagree, the culture of British menswear – and by this I don't mean all that trad Made in Britain bollocks that means nothing, or daft fancy dress stuff you see at London Fashion Week, or on the telly, I mean the genuine culture of British menswear – normal guys who like good product and spend money. Those guys have always been influenced by music and football, whether they know it now or not. It's ingrained in the UK.

The internet has a massive influence on the way we dress today – is this really a good thing?
Yes, people now know how to fold a fucking pocket square.

Would it be fair to say the internet has also been responsible for brands placing a much greater emphasis on marketing?
Brands have always put emphasis on marketing, it's just now they can do it differently. It also gives smaller brands the chance to reach out and connect with people. Surely that's a good thing?

Ironically, despite the rise of the internet, there has been a real resurgence in menswear print magazines in recent years. It's refreshing to see publications, such as *The Rig Out*, which provide something tangible with a bit of depth...
People will always like print.

Heritage is dead now, allegedly. What next?
Is it? Bollocks *shaves off tache*. Truthfully, it was dead before it began. Fancy dress costume for people with no opinion.

How many brands that provide 'classic menswear styles with a contemporary cut' does the world really need? We've seen the saturation of the streetwear market – is menswear heading in the same direction?
At the end of the day, you can't reinvent the wheel when it comes to men's clothes. The only thing you can really alter is the details. There are still a lot of creative designers and brands out there pushing things forward.

What do you look for in a brand, either as a consumer or as someone you could potentially work with?
As a consumer – something either very classic or difficult to acquire. To work with – someone either doing something genuinely creative or someone who is willing to pay for good work.

You do a fair bit of styling. Give us a style tip so we can all dress well.
It's all about confidence.

TELLASON

Tony Patella says the essence of his brand, Tellason is 'that we are not in fashion. We believe that people should care about where the products they buy are made and about the provenance of the components.'

Proudly Made in the USA, Tellason represents a craft-driven approach to clothing that blossomed after the recession and reinvigorated interest in the heritage and legacy of American manufacture. Rather than copy old garments, brands in this niche drew liberally from the past to create new products with a reverence for quality. Experience breeds perfection, and the idea of creating fresh lines is rooted in an interest in sustainable consumer and producer interaction.

Founded in 2008, Tellason is a joint venture by Patella – who cut his teeth during the 1990s as a partner in legendary denim man Cliff Abbey's young men's line Sutter's – and garment sales veteran Pete Searson. Their aim is simple: to entice people to believe in their purchases and buy less rubbish – to buy better rubbish (less often). The result is a line of denim, growing from a single original cut to five fits, built from meticulously sourced materials.

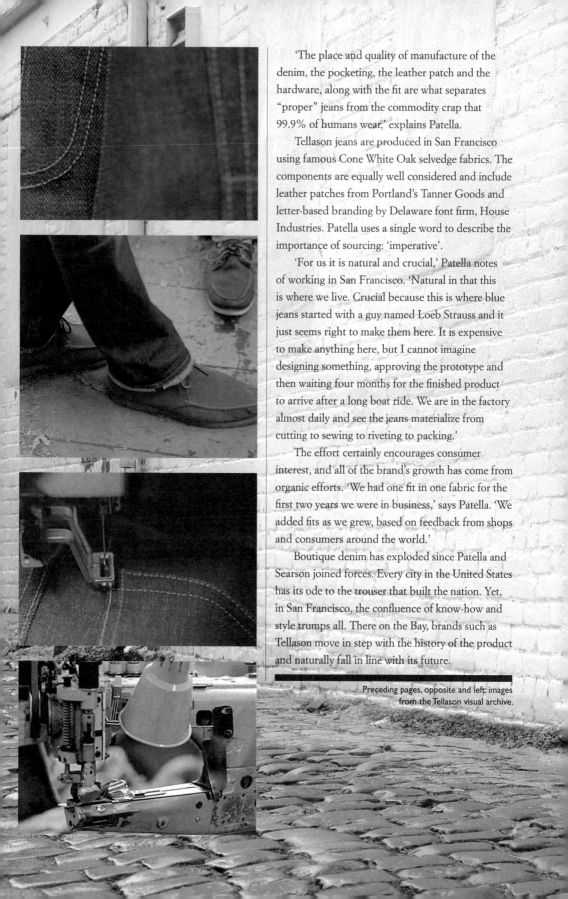

'The place and quality of manufacture of the denim, the pocketing, the leather patch and the hardware, along with the fit are what separates "proper" jeans from the commodity crap that 99.9% of humans wear,' explains Patella.

Tellason jeans are produced in San Francisco using famous Cone White Oak selvedge fabrics. The components are equally well considered and include leather patches from Portland's Tanner Goods and letter-based branding by Delaware font firm, House Industries. Patella uses a single word to describe the importance of sourcing: 'imperative'.

'For us it is natural and crucial,' Patella notes of working in San Francisco. 'Natural in that this is where we live. Crucial because this is where blue jeans started with a guy named Loeb Strauss and it just seems right to make them here. It is expensive to make anything here, but I cannot imagine designing something, approving the prototype and then waiting four months for the finished product to arrive after a long boat ride. We are in the factory almost daily and see the jeans materialize from cutting to sewing to riveting to packing.'

The effort certainly encourages consumer interest, and all of the brand's growth has come from organic efforts. 'We had one fit in one fabric for the first two years we were in business,' says Patella. 'We added fits as we grew, based on feedback from shops and consumers around the world.'

Boutique denim has exploded since Patella and Searson joined forces. Every city in the United States has its ode to the trouser that built the nation. Yet, in San Francisco, the confluence of know-how and style trumps all. There on the Bay, brands such as Tellason move in step with the history of the product and naturally fall in line with its future.

Preceding pages, opposite and left: images from the Tellason visual archive.

FILSON

C.C. Filson's story is pure American dream. Born in 1850, he travelled across the United States from his home state of Nebraska as a conductor on the rapidly expanding rail system. Eventually he reached Seattle, a small city in the Pacific North-west, which was gaining a foothold as a starting-point for other fortune hunters thanks to the great Alaska Gold Rush.

Filson didn't join the throngs moving to the Klondike looking for gold, but capitalized on their needs. In 1897, he opened C.C. Filson's Pioneer Alaska Clothing and Blanket Manufacturers. Specializing in hard-wearing goods, Filson's developed a lasting following, which continued beyond the Gold Rush when he received US Patent #1088891 for a trademark garment, the Filson Cruiser, in 1914.

'TO OUR CUSTOMERS: if a man is going North, he should come to us for his outfit, because we have obtained our ideas of what is best to wear in that country from the experience of the man from the North – not merely one – but hundreds of them,' wrote Filson in 1914. 'Our materials are the very best obtainable, for we know that the best is none too good and that quality is of vital importance. YOU CAN DEPEND ABSOLUTELY

UPON OUR GOODS BOTH AS TO MATERIAL AND WORKMANSHIP.'

Naturally, Filson's drive to make the best continued to convince hunters and outdoors men of the brand's great worth. When heritage became more than a word, mutating into a movement, Filson was perfectly positioned to join the American-made zeitgeist. Along with the Cruiser, retailers gravitated to the brand's rugged field bags and proprietary Tin Cloth fabric. The combination of universally handsome aesthetics and a remarkable American story made Filson the perfect poster brand for reigniting interest in homegrown looks and manufacture.

Teaming with Levi's in 2010, Filson solidified its legacy in the history of American workwear. Drawing from the archives of the better known labels, the collaboration reworked the iconic Levi's trucker jacket with Tin Cloth and Cruiser jacket-inspired pockets. In and of itself, the piece became an icon of contemporary menswear: a lesson in how to appropriate the past authentically for a new audience and entice consumers through studied design.

Roughly a century after patenting the Cruiser jacket, Filson embraced its balance of technical and traditional wears by repositioning its fits. With the introduction of the 'Seattle Fit', the brand recognizes that its new consumers value the same call for quality as the traditional 'Alaska Fit', but want it to have a different function. Slimming down silhouettes, Filson doesn't damage authenticity. Instead, the brand, still happily making bags and coats in Seattle, champions its own story and relishes an opportunity to stake a new foothold in American menswear.

While a Filson-made coat will still power through a Klondike winter, it'll also serve with style and panache from New York to Tokyo.

Preceding pages: Filson's iconic hunting jacket and a bag; above: the brand's London store; opposite: vintage archived garments.

MARK McNAIRY
NEW AMSTERDAM

Mark McNairy is a rule breaker. However, as he's quick to point out, 'you need to know the rules to bend them.' McNairy is not always overly verbose: asked where he learned the rules, he responded simply 'along the way'.

Born in Greensboro, North Carolina, McNairy graduated from an obsession with sneakers and athletic clothing to searching thrift stores for old Brooks Brothers Oxfords and vintage military khakis: 'There was nowhere else interesting to shop where I'm from.' McNairy's consumption gave him insight into the casual American garments, referred to in the trade as sportswear, and the basis for a career in fashion. 'My background is very much in sportswear,' he says. 'Sportswear is not athletic. Sportswear is unconstructed, the garments are made inside out. A tailored garment is made from the outside.'

Before sportswear, however, came women's clothing. 'My aesthetic and whatever has been consistent. I was doing men's clothes for girls,' says McNairy. 'After that, I started 68 and Brothers, which was very much replicating vintage American sportswear. I started McNairy Brothers at the same time, which is much the same as I'm doing now except I was only selling to Japan. I wanted to do tailored clothing, but hadn't had the opportunity.'

In 2005, opportunity came knocking. McNairy was signed up as creative director of venerable American (but Japanese-owned) brand J. Press. 'They hired me to bring a younger customer, because all of theirs were dying, literally,' he explains. 'Basically, my motto was step back to move forward. I wasn't trying to bring anything new, just trying to bring it back to where it used to be.'

Using the company's archives, McNairy began to employ an approach that would ultimately inspire a wave of contemporary designers: 'stepping back to move forward'. Looking at history and heritage to establish a contemporary look, working within the bounds of a brand to resuscitate interest.

McNairy did this and did it early. Before the heritage boom he was heralded, in 2006, for helping to revive prep.

'I wasn't trying to be innovative. Fit at J. Press, at the time, was part of it. The quintessential J. Press suit is a three-button sack suit, with no waist suppression,' McNairy notes. 'I was trying to bring in a two-button peak label, which for them was like "whoa, insane", but if you look back in the archives, they had it.'

Now, McNairy pushes buttons. 'My interpretation of Ivy League is more punk,' he says. 'I'm coming at it with a rebellious attitude.'

That attitude is present in his eponymous clothing and footwear line, Mark McNairy New Amsterdam. Mixing a colour blocking associated more with sneakers than formal shoes, he's worked with English manufacturer Sanders to create out-there versions of familiar silhouettes – covering longings and tassel loafers in camouflage and animal prints or mixing materials. He made wearing monk straps casually popular. In essence, McNairy has subverted tradition and turned the rules of prep inside out.

The rebellious streak extends to his design ethos. 'I'm not pushing a look,' he says. 'My clothes look different because of the process. I find imperfections attractive.'

McNairy bristles at looks he believes are 'outfits'. He doesn't stand for fashion. Instead, he makes pieces imbued with an inimitable humour, which function as odes to an old way of making and selling and a new way of thinking about what fits within the rubric of traditional American sportswear.

Preceding pages and opposite: Autumn/ Winter 2012/13; overleaf: McNairy's brash, modern take on preppy.

BIG JOHN

Big John, a Japanese denim brand, comes, like several Japanese denim brands, from a manufacturing company called Maruo Clothing, which has a long history in producing clothing. In the 1940s, Kotaro Ozaki started a sewing business to cater for the growing demand for non-traditional Japanese clothing, focusing on utilitarian, functional workwear as well as American-influenced clothing. Today, it seems like a natural step for it to have included jeans and, as the story goes, that is exactly what happened. By 1964 the first Made in Japan jeans under Canton Brand/Maruo Clothing and, almost simultaneously, the brand Big John were born. At the time, they even used cotton from the now infamous Cone Mills in America. From then on, Big John progressively became an underground hit, valued for the high quality of its denims. Despite not being the most famous of Japanese denims, Big John maintains this reputation to this day among those in the know.

Expert Japanese craftsmanship, Autumn/Winter 2013.

Above: Before and after wear on raw denim; opposite: Autumn/Winter 2013/14.

MAIDEN NOIR

Maiden Noir is not the first brand to capitalize on the utilitarian beauty of military-inspired clothing, nor will it be the last. However, each piece is executed with great aplomb. While M-65s and khakis may be ubiquitous, they are rarely done well. Maiden Noir draws heavily from vintage military pieces and reinterprets them from a contemporary standpoint to give the consumer something quite timeless.

Nin Truong founded Maiden Noir in Seattle in 2005. The brand functions as an offshoot of his design house, WKND, which is involved in everything from work with Nike to architectural design. Maiden Noir is just one of the many ways in which Truong exhibits his artistic tendencies. His ability to marry streetwear staples with functionality has seen the brand receive plaudits and secure stockists throughout America, Europe and Asia.

№ 7

Opposite: Autumn/Winter 2012/13;
overleaf: Autumn/Winter 2013/14.

JAPANESE MENSWEAR

by Calum Gordon

——— WWW.THEREFERENCECOUNCIL.COM ———

Calum Gordon is a Glasgow-based writer and editor-in-chief for The Reference Council. He has written for *Hypebeast* magazine and *Jocks & Nerds* magazine and has a keen and critical eye. Aside from being one of the co-authors of this book, he also works together with Steven Vogel on a number of projects.

I t would be remiss of us not to mention Japanese menswear as facet of menswear that is highly influential and yet somewhat cloaked in mystery. Without attempting to give it an imaginary subversive quality, there is certainly an obsession with all things Japanese within the realm of menswear, despite it being, for the most part, a sub-culture with which most consumers have not had any meaningful encounters. Beyond thumbing through a copy of *Free and Easy* or owning a pair of Japanese selvedge denims, there are few 'non-industry' people who have encountered Japanese menswear first hand, but for some reason many of us still harbour a complete and unyielding obsession with brands from Japan. I suspect this could partly be attributed to the apparent ability that the Japanese have simply to do things better than their Western counterparts. Then, again, that may be a complete over simplification of things. To begin to understand Japanese menswear, a beast quite unlike its contemporaries, requires an examination of where its strengths lie, what contributes to its unique standing and the perceptions and misconceptions surrounding these.

The world we inhabit is one engulfed in hyper-critical tendencies. This book will no doubt be criticized for certain inclusions and omissions in terms of brands and subject matter. Their criticisms may be valid, but it won't have been something we haven't considered and then ruled out due to the impracticalities of it. This somewhat brief exploration of Japanese menswear, alongside a small selection of Japanese brands, is merely a snapshot of a culture that remains relatively alien to outsiders and extremely guarded in terms of how they mould their reputation. This book is by no means exhaustive in how it examines Japanese menswear, nor menswear as a whole for that matter. However, the mystique that the Japanese facet is shrouded in requires much more digging in order to gain some semblance of what this scene is about. Partly, this is due to the fact that these brands have little need for a strong Western consumer base, such is demand in their homeland. For most retailers throughout the United States and Europe, brands such as WTAPS, Neighborhood or Kapital are desirable merely for the kudos of stocking them. These hard-to-obtain and often expensive brands make the shops very little money, but serve as a beacon to consumers and give the shop a level of prestige that is hard to attain otherwise.

The perception of Japanese quality falls in line with the age-old adage of 'there's no smoke without fire'. For the vast majority of brands within Japanese menswear, their quality is often unparalleled, as the likes of Visvim create products that would rival luxury brands such as Hermès both in terms of price and craftsmanship. Coupled with the almost excessive attention to detail that is exhibited throughout most Japanese collections is the ability to take clothes associated with Americana and improve them. While there are countless Western brands whose modus operandi is to 'reinterpret classic style from a contemporary standpoint', what most of them really mean is that they take a vintage style and make the silhouette slimmer and maybe even change a button or two. Without wishing to seem disingenuous to many Western brands, there are vast numbers of their Japanese peers who seem to go the extra step when it comes to such reinterpretations of past styles. Perhaps this willingness not only to improve the cut, but also to innovate beyond this point is where much of the allure lies in these brands.

In recent years, 'Japanese' has become a by-word for quality. Again, it stems from an obsession held by consumers and industry heads alike with Japan that has allowed brands to capitalize on our conceptions, or perhaps misconceptions. Apply the word Japanese as a pre-fix to your product's fabric and you are effectively saying that you have a superior product. In the same regard, Made in China automatically conjures up thoughts of poor working conditions and even poorer quality garments. These connotations are, quite simply, false. It propagates the idea of poor stitching and cheap materials and is ironically contrasted with the charming ideal of Japanese artisans who craft a single shirt a day from organic cotton picked by the seamstress themselves. It's all wrong, or rather, it's simply not black and white like that. Brands such as White Mountaineering and Nanamica, widely considered to be at the forefront of technical menswear apparel, both use Chinese manufacturers, and even the most renowned figure in Japanese menswear, Hiroki Nakamura, has certain shoes from his seminal Visvim line hand-sewn and crafted in China. If it is fair to say that Chinese production does not necessitate poor quality, the converse could be said of Japanese production. It is a word that has become one of the most effective marketing tools in menswear.

The idea of anything hailing from Japan being of a guaranteed high quality is, of course, partly attributable to the fact that it is true for many brands. This notion of quality, however, is reinforced by a price point far higher than the norm for niche menswear goods. There are certain economic factors at play, such as import tax and customs duties. Granted, this is not the only contributable factor to such prices, but there is undoubtedly a conscious decision on behalf of these brands to mark up prices. Without wishing to delve into Western consumer habits and psychological-based marketing ploys, these inflated prices do not act as a deterrent to the consumer. The exclusivity denoted by such prices perfectly manipulates those of us who, to varying degrees, indulge in sartorial one upmanship.

In a similar nature to retailers, there are nods of approval reserved for those who have gone to the trouble of attaining Japanese products, either through an extremely healthy bank balance or a Japanese proxy service – quite often both. Relatively little is known about these brands, save for a few obsessives, in comparison to Western brands and the half-truths and myths inevitably spread to create levels of desirability that are almost exclusively reserved for the unfamiliar. This somewhat mystical unattainability arguably stems from a culture that was fostered before the internet engulfed the world of fashion. There was a time, believe it or not, before cross-continental homogeny when it was nigh on impossible to have a wardrobe filled with Japanese brands while living somewhere in Middle England. The desire was undoubtedly there, thanks to a host of what we've come to know as 'influencers', but the means to this end were severely limited. While James Lavelle's BAPE snowboarding jacket in the 1998 video for UNKLE's Guns Blazing was the subject of complete fixation for many, the same fanatics also resigned themselves to the idea that they'd never own such a piece. It is this sort of mindset that has heavily contributed to the desirability of Japan's finest streetwear-cum-menswear brands.

While quality, or perceived quality, hype and desirability have all helped fashion this sub-culture that is fetishized by Westerners, it would be ignorant to omit the factor that draws many to practise such fetishes in the first place. The aesthetic element, which all clothes boil down to, is integral to our understanding of Japanese menswear. While the aforementioned ability to breathe fresh life into Americana is true of many brands, there are also a slew of brands that excel in terms of innovation, both in terms of fabric, construction and silhouettes. The likes of Rei Kawakubo and Yohji Yamamoto have witnessed a trickle-down effect of their work from the last 30 years, leading to a new generation eager to create garments that deviate from the norm. This does not necessarily require these brands to produce avant-garde fashion, but the design process of brands such as The Soloist and Undercover is one that is based upon innovation, evolution and the methods of garment deconstruction as championed by Comme des Garçons in the late 1980s. These brands harness these tenets in striving to create something genuinely new. Even brands such as Neighborhood and WTAPS, once considered 'streetwear' brands, have embraced such evolution to the point that their product speaks to a more grown-up, menswear-inclined audience today. Aesthetically, the Japanese not only often provide new perspectives on fresh ideas, but they do it in a thoroughly non-blasé manner which merely serves to add to the culture's mystique.

So, why do we treat these brands so differently? Why can Comme des Garçons demand £300 for a shirt, but a brand such as Nom de Guerre is forced to cut its prices by 30 or 40 per cent just to remain competitive? It is a culmination of factors that encapsulate psychology, ingenuity, quality and marketing. Yet, such reasons seem barely to scratch the surface of what makes Japan so different compared to the rest of the world. Maybe this is an unfulfilling discussion because you would need to devote a whole book to the subject just to get a handle on it from a Western perspective. The Japanese, despite what you may infer from this article, are not necessarily better at fashion, they merely approach it from an entirely different perspective, as do their consumers. We can try and get a piece of the pie because, at the end of the day, they are just clothes that often look great, but the wider culture will remain at odds with the way we view things.

S.N.S. HERNING

The city of Herning was established in the early 1800s. As the population of the Midtjylland region of Denmark grew, the town soon became a focal point for commerce. Despite being relatively small, Herning made its name from its proficiency in the textile industry. Nowadays, there are few remnants of the once thriving industry. Like many other once great textile towns, mass consumption and cheap foreign labour have consigned Herning's textile history to the past. There is, however, one exception to this sad decline that continues to carry the torch for the town of Herning.

S.N.S. Herning have spent over eight decades providing Danes with some of the most hard-wearing knitwear ever made to guard against Scandinavian winters. Once a ubiquitous household name, S.N.S. Herning is now a revered menswear staple for many. Simply put, their quality is near unrivalled and, in an age where origin and authenticity are of heightened importance, the brand has repositioned itself as an attractive proposition for those who appreciate a well-made product that is not readily available.

At the age of 32, Søren Nielsen Skyt combined his initials with the name of his hometown to create S.N.S. Herning. Skyt had spent his teenage years pedalling knitwear to fishermen and pretty much anyone who wished to guard against the harshness of the Danish winter. Traditionally, these fishermen would wear three sweaters at one time, with the oldest on the outside. Each year they would throw away the oldest sweater and buy a new one to be worn as an inner layer. The bitter conditions the fisherman faced meant a market existed for warm but lightweight knitwear.

Opposite: Autumn/Winter 2013/14; below, left: brand founder Søren Nielsen Skyt; bottom: the original S.N.S. factory, which is still used to this day; below, right: factory machine blueprint.

S. N. S.
HERNING
INDREGISTR. VAREMÆRKE

Skyt's eyes were opened to the technique of 'bubble knitting' in the 1920s. It provided superior insulation in comparison to many other knitting techniques and later became a trademark of Skyt's work. In light of this newly learned technique, Skyt purchased a jacquard knitting machine. These machines had to be imported from either England or Germany. The investment in this technology came to mould his eponymous brand. The fisherman sweater became the brand's most recognizable and revered item, one that is still manufactured to the same exact specifications to this day.

In days gone by, it was a rite of passage for any Dane to own a fisherman sweater. In the 1970s, almost every Danish child owned a Herning knit or some form of imitation. The staggering total of 150 domestic stockists has somewhat diminished since then. The decline in demand for Herning knitwear forced the brand to reinvent itself. Today, nearly half of the brand's stockists hail from outside Scandinavia. Very much still a family business, the S.N.S. Herning mill continues to be active in the town of Herning and is manned by the founder's grandson and namesake. Søren and his team of five highly skilled artisans continue to provide some of the finest knitwear available.

As touched on previously, we live in an age where the proverbial wheel has been reinvented and reinterpreted to the point that, for many, menswear became painfully mundane. As brands sought to out-gaud one another, the savvier consumer began to rediscover a love of simplicity and craft. Of course, in some cases, this desire to be authentic went too far and became a fad: the antithesis of the timelessness many consumers had reached for. That said, plenty of good came from the 'heritage' movement: imposters were left behind to look like a sad parody of what was once cool, people expanded their horizons and, most importantly, rediscovered an affinity for products with no expiration date. S.N.S. Herning's fisherman sweater is the epitome of this and an example of a truly great product that can largely remain undiscovered beyond the confines of territorial borders. It is brands such as S.N.S. Herning, decades old yet new to many, that provide the incentive for constantly seeking new, well-made products.

Preceding pages: Spring/Summer 2014 (shot by Kirstin Kerr), factory machinery (centre); opposite: Spring/Summer 2014 (shot by Kirstin Kerr).

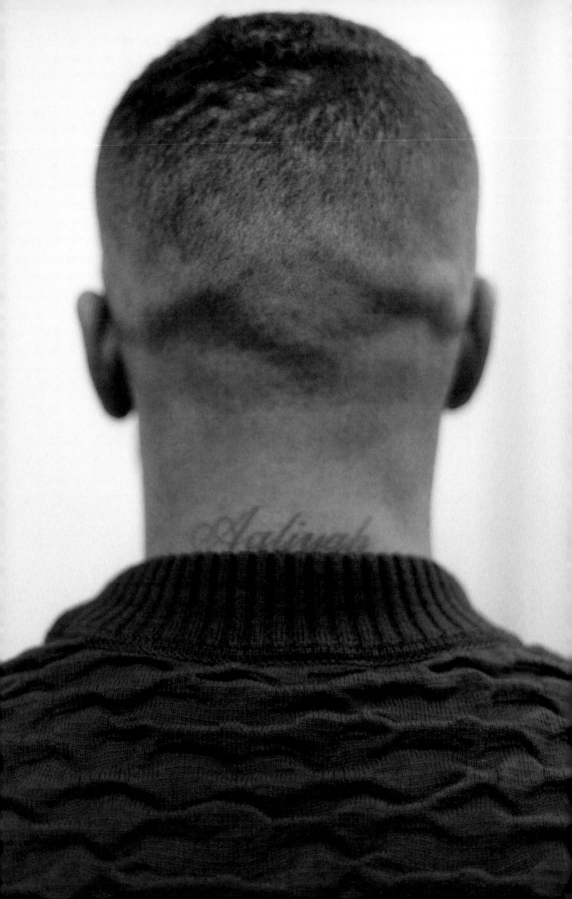

ARC'TERXY
VEILANCE

( )ne of the most interesting
contemporary trends is the fusion of technical
apparel production and traditional urban
sportswear. Bonded seams find form in trench coats
and backcountry-tested Gore-Tex membranes
push these garments beyond the limits of their
stylistic forefathers. Groundbreaking technologies
have been recast for the distinct challenges of the
urban environment and men with a passion for
performance product no longer need to dress like
weekend warriors.

Arc'teryx began life in 1989 as Dave Lane's
Rock Solid Manufacturing, with a firm focus on
rock-climbing harnesses. Two years later, Rock Solid
was rebranded Arc'teryx and the Vancouver-based
company took top harness honours. Attention to
perfection remained when Lane left in 1995. Designer
Mike Blenkarn joined and Arc'teryx shifted to the
development of Gore-Tex outerwear. Debuted in
1997, an advanced selection of alpine outerwear,
employing water-tight zippers, tapped seams and
laminate fabric, defined the future of Arc'teryx and
stamped the brand's industry-leading position.

The brand operates with a rather simple
ideal: 'At Arc'teryx, to challenge what exists and
manufacture new ideas is the culture.' Curiosity

matched with passion fuels design initiatives built on the belief that constant refinement breeds function-led solutions to the creation of products. Testing is done by both designers and athletes, ensuring that the process of design incorporates all potential usage and evolves with a disciplined approach according to the most unforgiving environments.

With Veilance, Arc'teryx expands brand appeal and applies knowledge and technological skill to a new set of challenges. While the products don't face the same rigours, they are built with the same commitment to excellence and expectations. It is performance menswear, designed and manufactured just like the alpine goods in Vancouver.

As consumers seek authenticity, sub-brands such as Veilance achieve a near impossible balance: working at once in step with contemporary needs, while simultaneously offering products that easily function beyond their intended purpose. The key is incorporating heritage – defined by design ethos – in an attempt to meet new, more stylish challenges. Contemporary menswear succeeds in blending approaches from different disciplines. Veilance succeeds through bringing backcountry-tested technologies to windswept, cross-town commutes.

Opposite, right and overleaf: Autumn/ Winter 2013/14.

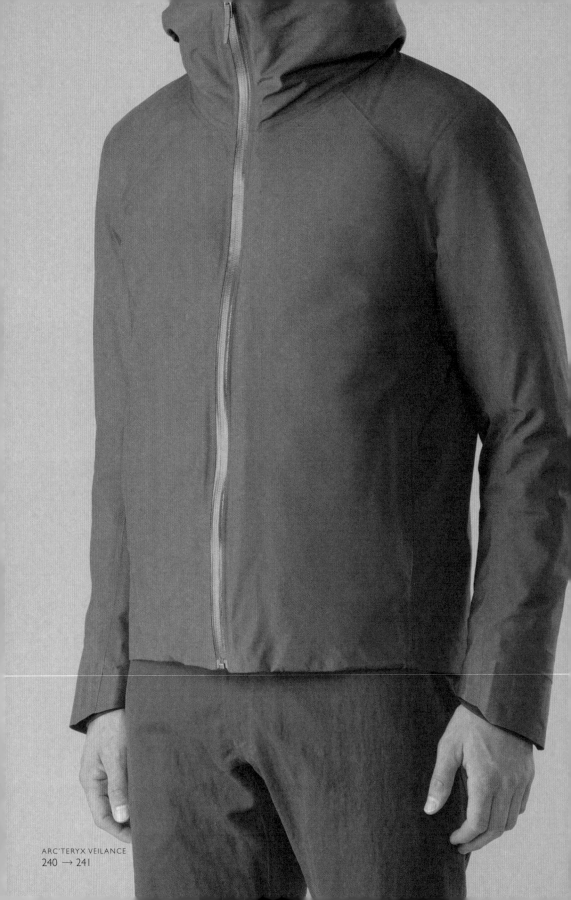

ARC'TERYX VEILANCE
240 → 241

UNIVER
WORKS

Ⅎ irst conceived in 2008 by David Keyte, Universal Works released its inaugural collection little under a year later with the aim of presenting a contemporary perspective of British menswear to a worldwide audience. Aesthetically, the brand draws from the varied life experiences of its founder, who worked in a Midlands coal mine wearing real workwear, not bastardized menswear iterations, before cutting his teeth at the likes of Paul Smith and Maharishi. His grounding in menswear provided the direction for how Universal Works would look: combining the elegance of Paul Smith with the brasher street-led sensibilities of Hardy Blechman's label.

Universal Works functions as an independent brand and has gained international, if not quite universal, recognition in recent years. Keyte's vision of being stocked on multiple continents is one that has come to fruition. The label is still intrinsically British, which is apparent in much of its offerings, but successfully manages to avoid the stereotypical stiffness that has plagued so many British brands. It is neither over-designed nor flashy. It is from such understatedness that the brand draws its versatility.

Right and opposite: Spring/Summer 2013; overleaf: Autumn/Winter 2013/14.

SAL

EBBETS FIELD FLANNELS

Decades before nostalgia and heritage became standard marketing ploys in men's clothing and when Made in the USA was dying rather than resurging, Brooklyn-native Jerry Cohen just wanted a stage uniform: he was in a rock band. Obsessed with sports logos and uniforms as a kid, Cohen's passion took full hold in 1987 when his desires met a roadblock. 'I started the company because no one was making what I wanted to buy (at the time it was a real wool vintage baseball shirt),' said Cohen. 'So, really, I didn't have a choice if I wanted to get one.'

A year later, after dutifully hunting down the proper vintage wool flannel, and after unexpected reactions from folks who saw Cohen in his jersey, Ebbets Field Flannels (named after the Brooklyn Dodgers stadium) was born. He focused on forgotten moments, celebrating the stories and designs that coloured America's non-major-league fields. EFF remade Negro League jerseys. The brand also reintroduced memories of the famed Pacific Coast League (which folded in 1958). With each step, the breadth of design increased, and slowly but surely fans flocked through EFF's mail order catalogue.

In 1990, Cohen received his first major press, a full-page look in *Sports Illustrated*. Along with a fellow sports fanatic, Peter Capolino, Cohen pioneered a phenomenon. Baseball started to 'turn back the clock', honouring the game's past style in special games. Naturally, Cohen helped dress the teams. His unmatched knowledge of baseball style played a valuable role in ensuring authenticity. Cohen has dressed actors in film and TV, and the New York Yankees on closing day of the original Yankee Stadium.

While Cohen's importance to the sports world – equally as an archivist and a producer – is undeniable, his role in maintaining and supporting traditional manufacture is less celebrated. In recent years, EFF has had a natural return to public consciousness, and not just for reproduction jerseys. As a new generation of consumer has championed well-made goods, the value of the great American baseball cap and perfect varsity jacket has returned. In step, Cohen's deep rootedness in classic 19th-century garments has helped many new upstart brands capture a piece of that history.

Around 2009, the menswear world rediscovered EFF and in 2010 J. Crew began

Opposite: Spring/Summer 2014.

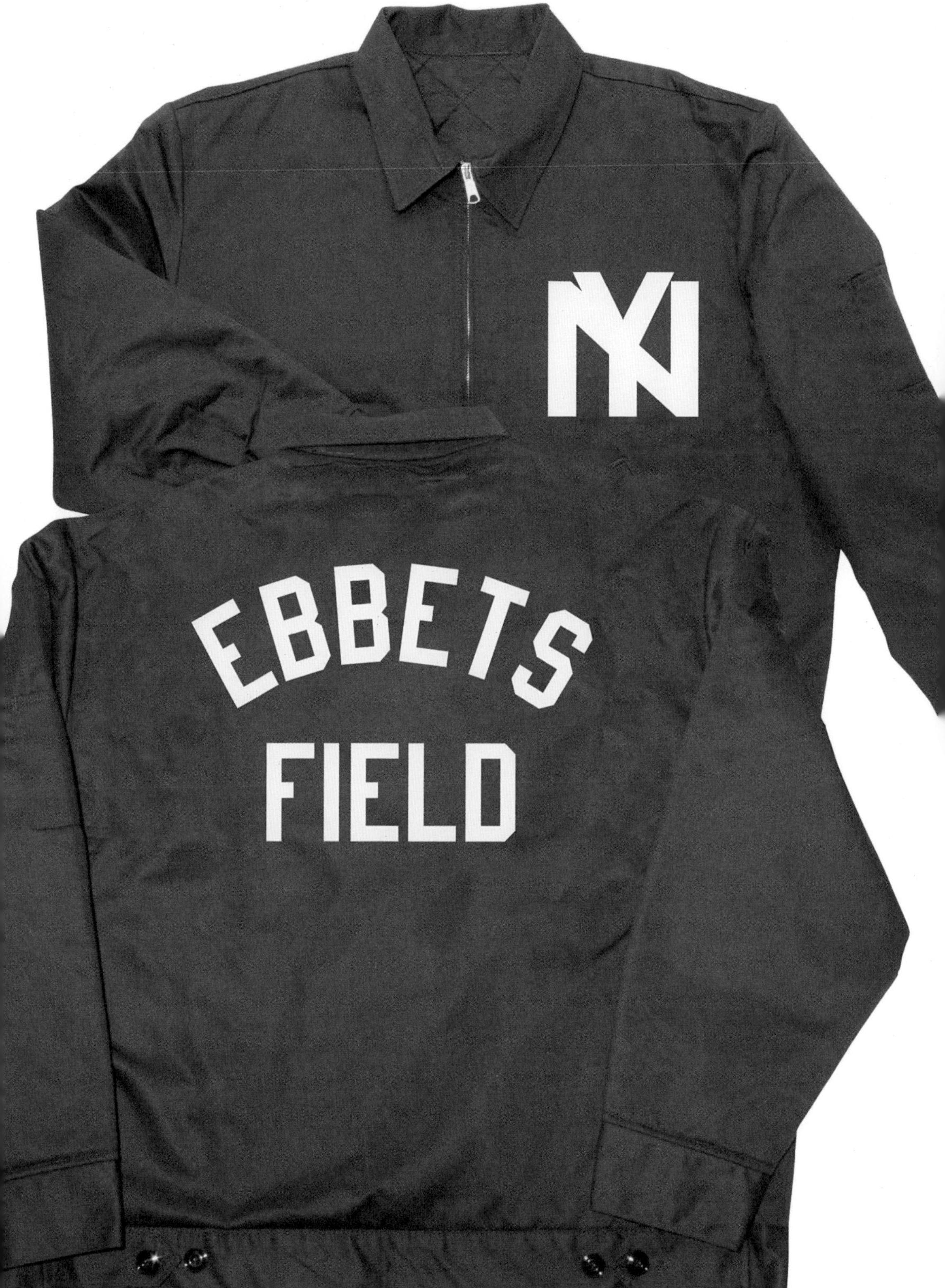
NY
EBBETS
FIELD

stocking caps as part of 'In Good Company'. This
put Cohen's product on a par with better known
brands such as Barbour and solidified the status of
its exemplary hats. The growth in brand recognition
dovetailed with renewed intrigue about the potential
of American manufacture. As new brands sprouted
around the country, Cohen became the go-to for
branded hats for everyone from independent upstart
denim artisans and Japanese repro companies to
savvy streetwear labels.

'The reaction is an absolute delight. We really
didn't do anything different, as we were doing our
thing for over 20 years. But it's great to see that
"investment" in our vision finally begin to pay off.
A project that brought it full circle was of course
doing uniforms for the movie *42*,' said Cohen in
regard to menswear's interest in his brand. 'It's also
great to work with people we respect like Bathing
Ape, *Inventory* magazine, the Imogene + Willie
folks, Baldwin Denim, and lots of others.'

'Working with Ebbets allows us to create high-
end, American-made, limited-run products that
suit our brand and customer,' notes Pete Williams,
founder of Montreal-based streetwear brand Raised
by Wolves. 'The build and feel that comes with the
history, there's nothing quite like it.'

That build and history, cornerstone of EFF
since 1988, has pushed Cohen's slow expansion.
In celebration of 25 years of operation, EFF moved
into a new space in Seattle that brings design,
manufacture and marketing under one roof. Cohen
invested in new knitting machines, eager to expand
his output, but also to preserve a dying skill in
the United States. This impulse is at the core of
Cohen's business: he is not content with just making
products, he wants to maintain American industry
and inspire more people to do the same.

'I think showing that what we could do could
indeed be done in the United States has been very
gratifying,' says Cohen. 'Whenever we achieve our
vision and fabric, decoration, and labour come
together it is a real joy.'

From stage dreams to contemporary menswear,
the EFF lesson supports the fact that all the best
products come to fruition when drive and passion
meet in equal measure.

Opposite: Ebbet's array of vintage replicas.

MUTTO

Muttonhead is a unisex brand that blurs the lines between classic sportswear and streetwear, while incorporating elements of sartorial refinement. This makes it hard to categorize as a brand, but is thoroughly intriguing. Founded in 2009 in Toronto, the brand has garnered a loyal following, both at home and abroad, in its relatively short existence. Today, Muttonhead remains a relatively small-scale operation, but it is at the forefront of a burgeoning creative scene in Canada.

The brand has exhibited a steadfast commitment to Toronto-based manufacturing and a social consciousness that led to the production of a vast amount of its product from recycled or organic cotton. Muttonhead, while retaining its badass aesthetic, will perhaps be one of the brands to usher in a new era of clothing manufacturing that places greater importance on being ecologically responsible.

Opposite: Autumn/Winter 2013/14; overleaf: Spring/Summer 2013.

NHEAD

MUTTONHEAD
Made in Canada

MUTTONHEAD BELIEVES
PRACTICING FAIR TRA
AND MANUFACTURES
GARMENTS IN TORON
CANADA.
www.MUTTONHEADCOLLECT

XS S M L XL

WHAT DO YOU WANT TO BE WHEN YOU GROW UP?

by Mark Smith

——————— WWW.PROPERMAG.COM ———————

Mark Smith is an English-based writer and co-founder of *Proper* magazine. Since this bi-annual publication was founded, *Proper* has evolved into one of the most revered publications within British menswear. Smith's humorous but eloquent writing style has seen him work with the likes of Levi's, Oi Polloi and *Hypebeast* magazine.

'What do you want to be when you grow up?' It's the perennial question you get asked as a kid, isn't it? In my early years I was certain I'd overcome bad knees, crippling shyness and chronic asthma to become the next Johan Cruyff, or at the very least, his English Fourth Division counterpart. As I got older I stuck with the football, but the fact that I also stuck with the cakes, fast food and bad lungs meant I was never going to get anywhere near my dream. I didn't know what I wanted to be when I grew up. At school I was pretty average. I liked drawing, PE and history and that was about it. I never once thought I'd end up writing for money. My English teacher was called Mr Cook, a tardy, fey individual who instantly led us all to believe he was 'on the other bus', a rumour he scotched frequently by referring to his son and wife. Maybe he was on the verge of doing an Elton John – either way, he wasn't a good teacher.

When I reached 16, I was left in no doubt about what was expected of me. I was to get out there into the big wide world and earn my keep. I left school and joined a Youth Training Scheme where they gave me free leather boots and less than £40 a week to live on. This wasn't just after the Second World War, by the way, it was 1996. The four buses a day cost me half my wage. After a 55-hour week pretending to learn about engineering, I realized I had nothing in common with the people I was spending my days with. A low point for me (and them) was when they gave me a list of things to get from the wholesalers which included hilarious items such as rainbow-coloured paint and sky hooks. I collected my GCSE results the following Monday, signed up for two more years at school and then told the YTS I wasn't coming back. I kept the leather boots, though, and eventually sold them on eBay for more than I'd earned spending a week as a junior joey.

I still didn't know what I wanted to be when I grew up, though, so signed on to do a two-year business course. The highlight was when a kindly old economics teacher described me as 'enigmatic'. I had to look it up in a dictionary (remember them?) but was chuffed when I realized what it meant. Most of my two years was spent scribbling up awful, last minute essays on the bus to school and undertaking extensive (but non-existent) dental work, which necessitated a large number of full days away from school. The fact this spell coincided with my football team being the best it had ever been may have had a small hand in this. Football was still important to me.

I finally left school after seven years there, all told. I'd lived in Stockport, a town six miles from the centre of Manchester, but my school was a further 15 miles south in Macclesfield. With relations in and around Manchester, I ended up soaking up everything that would emanate from a city and slowly bleed outwards into the surrounding towns. This was before the internet took over the world and everything was organic. When I left school they still had original punk rockers in Macclesfield, whereas in Manchester everything all seemed very laddish. The late 1990s were the time when I really started to take a stronger interest in clothing and footwear and, when Adidas moved their UK HQ to Stockport, an obsession was born.

Meanwhile I worked in a number of mundane, awfully paid office jobs. I was no closer to deciding what I wanted to be when I grew up. It was in one of these office jobs that I first encountered a chap named Neil Summers. He bounded over to my workstation, with his uncommon shoulder-length hair momentarily disarming me. 'Can I borrow your pritt stick?' he asked, while pointing to my Bricanyl asthma inhaler. That shared joke somehow eventually grew into *Proper* magazine, via misuse of company IT (for which we both received a reprimand), lots of pissed-up nights out and a couple of trips abroad during which we challenged an entire nation to a fight on a dual carriageway, ate steak with Swedish and Mancunian menswear royalty in Paris.

Eventually my scribblings in *Proper* led to an association with the aforementioned Mancunians of Oi Polloi that still ebbs and flows to this day. As their own success story began another chapter in bigger premises and a new website, I was given the task of somehow evolving the amusing musings of OP founding father Steve Sanderson, writing newsletters and copy for their new website. I loved it, but I still didn't know what I wanted to be when I grew up.

I decided I'd rewind a little and go back to school to learn how to write properly. In keeping with my other short-lived grand plans, I lasted just one day on the course before my perceived desire to 'make summat of meself' opened a number of unexpected doors before me. *Proper* attracted the attention of *Loaded* Ladfather James Brown and for two issues it was to be assisted by him and a designer called Matt Sankey, something we never expected or sought but are glad happened. Oi Polloi also decided they would need me to write more words for them. Uni could wait. It's still waiting.

Proper continues with the help of a new designer, Mike Fallows. Without him, I'm not quite sure what *Proper* would look like, though it'd probably involve the use of that pritt stick Neil wanted to borrow all those years ago. Writing has also presented itself to me in the form of Levi's Vintage Clothing, Adidas Originals, Baracuta, UVU, various magazines, more for Oi Polloi, stuff for The Original Store. There's other stuff but I'm forgetful.

I enjoy it. I'd like to do more.

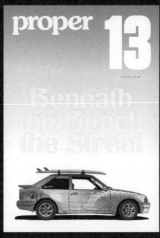

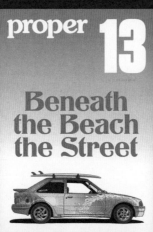

BILLYKIRK

I n 1999, brothers Chris and Kirk Bray hit on a simple way to match Kirk's fashion degree with the older Chris's business background: watch straps. Apprenticing under Arnold Arons, a third-generation leather worker, they set up Billykirk – the name comes from their father's nickname for Kirk whose full name is William Kirkland – and started selling straps and wallets out of Los Angeles. Soon after, they moved east to New Jersey, expanded their output to include bags and began working with American tanneries, including Pennsylania-based Wicket & Craig. Sourcing only domestic materials, the brand blossomed from one concerned with allowing Kirk an artistic outlet to a label with an overt concern for sustaining American jobs and minimizing environmental impact.

Unwittingly, through sheer interest in crafting an heirloom product, the Bray brothers set in motion a wider trend of smaller firms aiming to restore interest in American industry. Here, Chris explains how the brand has grown over its short existence and the challenges that face small, craft-based businesses.

How has Billykirk changed over time?
This reminds me of a Darwin quote: 'Natural selection acts only by taking advantage of slight successive variations; she can never take a great and sudden leap, but must advance by short and sure, though slow, steps.'

Billykirk is like an old oak tree and I think our slow growth has helped keep us relevant, approachable and somewhat resistant to change. That's actually an aspect of our brand that I am quite proud of, the fact that we really haven't changed over time. Sure we have developed more products in different categories and our business has grown, but we have not wavered from our original ethos – to design and create original, well-crafted items in the USA using superior materials. If you were to lay out everything we have produced over the last 13 years, there would be a continuity to it, which we both feel is extremely important to a brand's legacy.

Speaking of legacy, it wasn't long into our company's existence that we hit on the idea that our product would have to be timeless in design and needed to be made so well that the owner would want to pass the item down to their child. We loved this notion as it flew in the face of all the shoddily made, cheap merchandise that sat on many stores' shelves. This 'heirloom mentality' that we have been fostering for years now is something we are very proud of and I think is very relevant and unique in our current 'throw-away' society. In fact, we have received a number of testimonials regarding our heirloom belief and thanking us for making items that are made with pride and have integrity. We have also received a number of requests from parents specifically asking us to write a note of provenance to their child regarding the item, knowing that one day they will pass it down to them. This sort of connection is deeply moving and really helps to motivate us.

What do you learn from the heritage boom? How has the marketing of a craft product changed or stayed the same in the last five years?
Regarding the heritage boom, this is an interesting question and one I have a hard time wrapping my head around. One could look at the evolution of the Pop Up Flea as an example of this craft and heritage movement for some answers. There is no denying that Michael Williams and Randy Goldberg essentially helped engineer a re-adaptation of one of our most cherished of cultural narratives: the working-class hero toiling away with his or her hands, making something that they take great pride in. This is what founded our great nation and now has mythical status. The timing of this heritage boom was perfect but not exactly unfounded.

We have had 40 plus years of outsourcing, job loss, greed, waste and landfills bulging to last us all a lifetime. If you throw in the massive financial meltdown where millions lost their jobs, you then have a ton of people questioning things and many looking to the past for answers...to our heritage, in a sense. In the spirit of ingenuity, opportunity and resilience, many of these job seekers began to tinker in their basements and garages inventing things and crafting things. Cottage industries, aided by the internet and bloggers, were soon popping up every day. Along with all these invigorating, passionate pursuits, I think many parts of our society stepped back, took a look at their lives, their accumulated stuff and began to question it all. What many realized is what the original pioneers did, and that was to live within their means.

Whenever any sort of movement reaches a cult-like following and is marketed and hyped to death, I tend to shy away and move onto something else. However, this is different because it has a deep-seated element of pride attached to it, so when the hangers-on and groupies do fall away it will still be culturally relevant because of its myth-like foundations.

As the Pop Up Flea developed and expanded over the years, it was refreshing to see the attendees become more sophisticated each year. To have conversations with customers who genuinely care how an item is made, where it's made, and where the materials were sourced from was surprising.

This wasn't the case a few short years ago and I think it speaks about the resurgence and relevance of the craft community you ask about.

Not to get too far off onto a tangent but…this creative community was at one time intrinsically linked with the community in which one resided. There was a huge sense of pride that went along with it and rightly so. Craftspeople and artisans were revered in their community, all benefited and all were made better. I am not sure when this symbiotic and meaningful existence started to erode, but I assume greed had a lot to do with it, along with industrialization and modernization of trade and industry.

I am no historian or anthropologist, but somewhere along the way the 'blue collar' moniker started to get a bum rap. People in similar fields of craft that I am in were now seen as second-class citizens. Unfortunately, that perception and the onslaught of cheaper made products from overseas really took the sails out of many of those creative, hands-on style pursuits that were so prevalent at the turn of the century. On top of that, for over a century parents in an almost robotic fashion have all hoped to have children who will become doctors, lawyers or accountants. In other words, jobs that utilized one's hands lost their lustre and became belittled. So, in effect, this once vital and successful creative community has by and large been hugely assaulted by big business, greed and an ignorant arrogance.

Clearly there is a class and generational theme at play here. I know full well that my father's generation was hell-bent on their children setting roots within a big company, getting on their 401K plan and full health/dental coverage and plodding along working towards advancement within that organization for the next 35 plus years. To me that way of life is akin to rotting away. Sure, there was a time when job security meant just that, and this stereotypical father figure striking out to work each day in suit and tie for most of his life is simply one aspect of the American Dream. However, as a parent and small business owner engaged in a creative field, I find it very troubling. Is there anything intrinsically wrong with being a potter, welder or craft beer maker?

The horrible financial crisis was a huge watershed moment for a great many of us, and we are beginning to see a push for these older, more humble ideals as business models.... Growing our own crops, being better stewards of the earth, making our own clothes, on-shoring, thinking globally and acting locally.

Our hands are not just for eating and typing, and we are finding ways to be self-sufficient while producing something that not only pays our bills, but also helps our local communities. Websites such as Etsy are proving that getting a team of like-minded people in a community to work towards a common goal is not only possible but profitable. Billykirk is no exception and, like most in a cottage-style industry, we don't have shareholders breathing down our necks, cheapening and compromising our values and principles all for the almighty dollar.

What are the challenges of running a small business in this market?

There are a lot of challenges for us, but it usually revolves around credit. Banks, which were once eager to help with lines of credit, are now pulling on their purse straps real tight. The other issue is that producing goods in the US is tough. It primarily revolves around cost-of-living issues with our manufacturers and they're having to pay their workers a fair wage. We completely understand these challenges and have learned to adapt rather than sacrifice on quality. It's part of the domestically made landscape we find ourselves in.

Luckily, many of our items are being produced by a group of Amish leather workers in Pennsylvania. On the business side, they are about the best manufacturers to work with for a number of reasons. They are totally fair and honest people, they are extremely eco-friendly, they are very skilled – many have been honing their leather craft since they were boys while sitting on their father's knee. There is never a shortage of workers and, because of the way they live, they are virtually immune to the daily expenses that normal business owners and their employees have to deal with. They don't have cell phone or internet bills, they don't drive so there are no car insurance or gas expenses, they don't have

to dress their kids in the latest fashions and buy all sorts of sports equipment, they don't have TVs or tennis or music lessons to pay for, and they don't take expensive vacations that involve flying. They are totally self-sufficient and resourceful, so there are no plumber or electrician bills piling up, and in their later years there are no nursing homes or retirement community costs to fork out. It's a match made in heaven.

Beside capital and COG concerns, the other challenges are centred on growth, strategy and where to put our resources and energies. While we may be good designers and are able to read the market, we admittedly lack in other areas of business where a seasoned veteran could help guide the Billykirk ship. In overcoming these very important obstacles, we have reached out to a number of talented business vets and thankfully consider Mickey Drexler, the CEO of J. Crew, as one of the people who has been very helpful in mentoring us.

It's no surprise that many small business owners have challenges. But challenges keep us on our toes, constantly thinking and overcoming obstacles. However, I love being a business owner in a creative field where I can control my destiny.

How have collaborations helped amplify your business?

I think more than the collaborations themselves, it's the bloggers who get behind them and amplify their existence that have helped us the most. I will say, however, that collaborating with certain brands has helped get our feet into other demographics. Vans and Opening Ceremony, for example, are two stores that cater to customers who may never have heard of us until we began working together. The collaborations we have done with United Arrows and Journal Standard are great for us and get a ton of press. We also feel very fortunate to be aligned with Levi's and The Hudson's Bay Company because of their legacies and long-standing histories. Finally, our relationship with J. Crew has really helped expand our name recognition.

Opposite: crafted contemporary takes on classics.

BILLYKIRK

LEATHERMAKERS HANDMADE IN THE USA EST. 1999

INDIGOFERA

Indigofera Jeans is, as the name suggests, a denim brand. In addition to its Swedish heritage, the brand is extremely serious about making high-quality products akin to its Japanese counterparts. The majority of the products are made in Japan and Europe with Japanese fabrics, and it shows. Indigofera's drive to create the best possible products is noteworthy, and surprisingly uncommon. It is one thing to want to make the best product possible, but quite another actually to create it. Apart from the fantastic run of denims it makes, Indigofera also offers a great selection of tops, knits and jackets, as well as woollen blankets.

Left and opposite: from Autumn/Winter 2009/2010 until the present; overleaf: Spring/Summer 2010.

MONITALY

onitaly was founded in 1997 as a sister brand to the Japanese footwear label Yuketen. Using the same principles of craftsmanship and quality, along with design nuances that emanate from classic Americana styles, Yuki Matsuda's menswear line has gained much notoriety in recent years.

The brand takes its name from Matsuda's three greatest sources of inspiration: his daughter Monica, Italy and the military, or, more precisely, the quality of military spec clothing. Naturally, military styles are apparent in much of Monitaly's work, which comfortably sits alongside hunting- and sportswear-inspired garments. The collections themselves have tended to place an emphasis on hard-wearing outerwear and shirts, somewhat ironically for Matsuda, who resides in the warm climes of southern California. Yet, it is his fascination with vintage styles and durable fabrics that manifests itself in much of the brand's output.

Monitaly has been at the forefront of menswear in recent years, in part due to its Americana aesthetic, but also because the brand has provided a level of consistency that others have struggled to match. With each passing season, the offerings from Monitaly seem to expand while maintaining the same considered approach to construction and fabrics. The brand's philosophy, 'every stitch has a soul', truly encapsulates its attitude towards creating timeless garments.

Opposite: Autumn/Winter 2013/14; overleaf: Autumn/ Winter 2013/14 and Spring/Summer 2013.

EASTLAND

astland Shoe Mfg. Corp. was founded in 1955 by Jonas B. Klein, Bertram Wolfson and Louis Fishman in Freeport, Maine. At that time, the shoe manufacturing business in Maine was flourishing. In fact, the history of shoemaking in the state of Maine and the town of Freeport, in particular, dates back to the early 1800s when it was mainly a small cottage industry, with shoes being made for local consumption. As with many states in the north-east, Maine began its industrialization with cotton and textile mills along its major rivers, but with the evolution of the steam engine, shoe manufacturing was no longer tied to waterways and was able to extend its fingers into other parts of the state. As the US economy began to grow during the Industrial Revolution, so did the demand for shoes. In 1955, Eastland was one of five shoe manufacturers in the town of Freeport, with the original Eastland factory and corporate offices located at 6 Park Street, directly alongside the Pan Am Railways' tracks that run through the town.

Eastland was founded in 1955. What is the origin of the company?
Eastland began as a private label shoe manufacturer, making 900 pairs a day of beaded laced moccasins, and various handsewn styles for national and regional shoe stores at its Freeport factory. National chain stores such as Edison's, Thom McAn, Kinney and Endicott-Johnson, which are no longer in existence, as well as many other national wholesalers, provided the volume needed to build a strong factory base. Many of our competitors today, such as Sperry, Bass, Calvin Klein and FootJoy, at one point in time offered collections that were designed and manufactured by Eastland. At times, we even stitched uppers for some of today's leading athletic brands, and worked on special make-ups for the Boston Celtics.

Over the years, the company grew to be one of the largest independently owned shoe manufacturers in the United States, operating six facilities across the state of Maine: Eastland, in Freeport, a complete factory manufacturing 10,000 pairs a day, which housed the corporate offices up until 2004; Depot Street (also in Freeport), where the sole materials were cut, assembled and processed; Hunter Road, the location of the original distribution centre; Northland, in Fryeburg, Maine (started in 1964), where the uppers for the Freeport factory are cut and stitched, producing 3,000 pairs a day; Westland, in Biddeford Maine, where men's shoes

Preceding pages: the brand's iconic moccasins; above, right and opposite: archive photos from the brand's long history.

are manufactured; and a facility in Lisbon, Maine, where the uppers are cut and stitched for the Freeport factory, manufacturing 4,500 pairs a day. During the peak of the US manufacturing days, Eastland employed nearly 750 workers in a 60-mile radius around Freeport.

In the 1970s, as shoe manufacturing began to shift off-shore and less expensive imported footwear began to take a larger share of the private label domestic shoe business, we decided it was time to build our own brand and change our marketing strategy. At the same time in the 1980s, there seemed to be a very serious renewed interest in goods Made in the USA, especially shoes. As a family-owned and operated brand, we were able to control our pricing strategically to offer shoes that were both made in the USA and affordable compared to our competitors.

In the 1990s, building on the success of our classic styles, we began to build up our export business to Europe and focus on an already successful business in Japan and Canada. Every shoebox that left our factories proudly displayed 'Made in Freeport, Maine, USA'. By 1994, we were shipping millions of pairs of shoes to retailers around the world.

By the mid-1990s, more than 90% of all shoes purchased in the US were produced offshore. Even though the prices of our shoes moved beyond the levels that our retail partners could pay for them, we remained committed to manufacturing our products in Maine. To keep our three core factories and 750 employees healthy, we decided to supplement some of our line with shoes that we were not set up to make competitively in Maine. In 1998, we began importing a small amount of footwear from Brazil and China, primarily shoes that were styled more appropriately for the times. With the changing fashions of the 1990s, these styles began to sell well, and became more important to our customers than our traditional Maine-made items that we were known for.

In 2010, we celebrated Eastland's 55th anniversary. Much had changed during the course of our company's history. Unable to compete with our competitors who had began sourcing shoes overseas years before us, we closed the last of our factories on 18 September 2001. The company moved its corporate office from 6 Park Street to 4 Meetinghouse Road in Freeport, and resumed the business of selling Eastland branded shoes around the world.

To mark our 55th anniversary we decided to reintroduce a core collection of classic Eastland camp mocs, loafers and boat shoes, all manufactured in our home state of Maine. By partnering with the

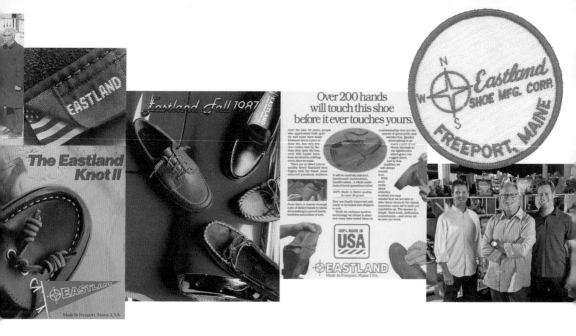

few Maine factories and facilities that still remained, we launched our Eastland Made in Maine collection in September 2010. It is currently available in some of the finest retailers around the world. We've carefully branded these shoes 'Made in Maine', a moniker that has since taken on a life of its own and is now used commonly by other brands and in the market. After some sixty years of offering Eastland shoes, it's nice to know that it still means something to be from Maine, just like us.

Maine is the epicentre of handsewn shoes in America. How did the industry develop in the state? How does Eastland fit into that history?
I've already touched briefly on how the industry developed in the state and, in particular, Freeport. I'd like to add that with a large number of footwear brands historically located in the north-east, presumably due to close proximity to the major cities, it makes sense that the surrounding areas would have reaped the benefits of these companies after the Industrial Revolution. Like any other industry, shoemaking has historically always been in search of the next location to make products and keep costs down. These companies would need a hard-working, plentiful workforce, outside of the major cities, which Maine was able to provide. I think the European and Canadian

immigrants settling in the state around this time also played an important part in bringing the industry to the state.

Maine's industry has been historically reliant on our forests for shipbuilding and lumber. Footwear and textiles have also always been important. Outside of agriculture and the logging industry, there wasn't an overabundance of job opportunities. Growing up in Maine, I can tell you that Mainers are hard-working, detail-oriented people, they're not afraid to get their hands dirty and they're proud of what they do. Shoemaking is a hands-on craft, and it's something the state is quite proud of.

I think another interesting piece of this can be seen if you think about the origins of the moccasin, which was present in the north-east before the Europeans arrived. Over time, this way of making shoes was adapted and updated. Our industry has modified the designs to be more practical for everyday use.

More importantly, I think in the case of Eastland, this practicality mirrors where we are from. Maine is a casual, laid-back, practical place with a long stretch of coastline and extensive forests. Our shoes reflect this, and in many cases incorporate this in handsewn details. I think the attraction of Maine draws people from out of state and we've built a brand around that.

I think Eastland is best known for the camp moc (as it stands, the Falmouth). Where do the classic New England styles come from?

Yes, our camp mocs have been a very important part of Eastland's history and are styles we've been making since the 1950s. The Falmouth and Yarmouth are styles that we plan always to have around. They've become iconic styles for us.

The camp moc comes from Maine. Every brand that has come and gone, and called Maine its home at some point in their history, offered a camp moc. As I've said, I think it represents a slice of Maine life: it's a bit nautical, it's a bit preppy, it's a bit rustic, it's durable and practical, it's classic and timeless. I think they were originally intended to meet the demands of a typical Mainer's life, to provide an everyday casual shoe for what Maine threw at them, from the rugged coasts and beaches, to the lakes, river and forests; sockless in the summer, and paired with heavy wool socks in the fall and winter.

There's an allure around camp mocs that I think appeals to people from away. They are familiar in appearance, but evoke a rustic lifestyle that's not part of their daily life. For people not from Maine, there's a bit of mystery surrounding them, they're intriguing.

What is the Eastland design process?

We have a design team in New York and in Maine that is responsible for all of our products. One thing we've learned with our Made in Maine collection is that people want products from us that tell a story and reflect our 57-year history. Our customer base for our Made in Maine shoes spans a wide range, from classic to progressive streetwear stores, which allows us to reach a wide audience of consumers. Each season, we are careful to have a mix of classic, understandable styles, as well as a selection of classic silhouettes with a unique, but subtle twist. Being a family-run company with employees who have been with us for many years, we have plenty of experience at the office to tap into. We spend a lot of time looking through our sample archives and old catalogues. The trick is updating items to be relevant for today's market.

The Made in Maine collection came during the 'heritage' boom. How important was it for Eastland to find a space in that market and re-establish position?

The 'heritage' boom was important for Eastland because we were able to bring something genuine and relevant to the table. As a family-owned company, we are literally telling our story, and I think people like making that connection. It opened new doors for us and, as a result, people are looking at our men's shoes more seriously. There are lots of brands today that are telling a Made in Maine story, but we're among the few remaining Maine shoe brands that really have this history. It was important for us to find a space in this market because this is our story.

As heritage becomes #menswear, are there any challenges in keeping up with trends while maintaining brand integrity? I love the camo collection. I'm interested in the process of making those shoes a reality.

This is certainly a challenge. As trends change and styles evolve, we have to come up with ways to stay relevant. We always say that one of the beauties of our company has been our ability to adapt and change over the years, but still remain true to what Eastland represents. We adapt to trends, but try to put a compelling story behind it. At this level, it has to be unique to get some attention, and it has to have a reason. The Realtree camo project was a good example of that – we wanted to incorporate camo into some of our classic styles, but still represent a Maine lifestyle.

What is the lasting legacy of the 'heritage' boom?

I think the lasting legacy of the 'heritage' boom is that it reaffirms the importance of being true to what your brand represents, while at the same time staying relevant and being patient. Americans are nostalgic and want to connect with brands, they want to know the story behind the product, and they want it to come from a reliable, dependable source.

Opposite: an archive photograph.

DEUS EX MACHINA

K ack in 2006, something crept out of the backwaters of Australia: the first brand to represent visually and aesthetically a whole new generation of what your girlfriend's parents warned her about.

Essentially, Deus Ex Machina is a custom motorcycle company and we could easily leave it at that, but there is so much more to be said. Unlike the 1970s bikers glorified by a bunch of mostly poor films, Deus represents and crafts a generation of enthusiasts who are not content simply to adopt the bike culture of years gone by; there is so much more to them. Deus reflects this: surfing, skating, friendship and freedom mixed with a goodly amount of rebellion are all part of the brand.

The Deus empire has extended with a killer store in Sydney, a hideout on Bali – essentially a recreational dream come true for many of its consumers – a significant store in Los Angeles and an international presence that seems unstoppable. Whether you like their bikes, clothes, art, parties or all of the above, it seems that everyone is welcome under their roof.

Opposite: Autumn/Winter 2013/14;
right: Spring/Summer 2013;
overleaf: Autumn/Winter 2013/14.

ON THE OBVIOUS OMISSIONS

Obviously, with any undertaking such as this book, which through a number of essays and brand profiles tries to bind a loosely associated scene under one moniker, there are going to be some omissions.

What we wanted to do was to unite the majority of independent brands within this book – that was the loose guideline we set for ourselves. Aside from the limitations such as the actual number of pages we had available for this, we made a few editorial decisions that are at best debatable. For example, why are A.P.C., Saturdays, Norse and 3sixteen not included in this book? Why is there a distinct lack of leading Japanese brands?

To shine a light on these editorial and sometimes plain boring realities, some brands, we all agreed, did not need to be in the book for such a large number of reasons that I have already forgotten them. Occasionally, a brand declined to be included,

again, for a number of reasons either so silly or important that I have forgotten them. Sometimes, a brand or its respective PR firm didn't answer our calls or emails. That can happen, but irrespective of those random, head-scratching omissions, I believe we paint a very colourful and informative picture.

It is the bigger omissions, some I've already mentioned in the introduction, that I want to speak about here: where are Levi's, Ralph Lauren, Red Wing, Alden, Comme des Garçons, Stone Island, J.Press and J.Crew?

As far as I am concerned, these brands, these empires, have in a way a lot to do with contemporary menswear, just like the brands we chose to cover in here. Arguably, some of those mentioned above even went as far as being absolutely vital in shaping and forming what we know as contemporary menswear these days. Especially, in my opinion, brands such as Ralph Lauren and J.Press. But does that mean we should align them in the same story as the other brands? I believe not, and as a matter of fact I believe Ralph Lauren deserves a few books just to itself, aside from the ones that already exist, and the same can and has been said about the Stone Island empire. Furthermore, as Nick put it: 'a lot of those brands were reinvigorated in the market, but production didn't change, nor did their outset.' This is really one of the main reasons why we chose not to cover those obvious giants in this field. In a way, I believe that these major brands piggy-backed on a trend created by small independents, which is their job, but, additionally, their presence is so overwhelming at times that they didn't need another piece of press for their PR department.

I naturally assumed that you, the reader, by simply choosing to pick this book up and read it, would already be aware of the above, but may not have put the collection of brands in here in the overall context as we have presented it.

So, don't be mad that you didn't see the millionth picture of the Red Wing factory in here. We have all seen those images more often than we need to, and, yes, I have several pairs and they are great boots, same as my two pairs of LVCs, but again that point is not even being debated here. Irrespective of these and other omissions, I do firmly believe that the collection of brands and opinions collated in here is as good as an overall representation of modern, independent and contemporary menswear as you can find.

Yours,
Steven Vogel

FURTHER READING

PRINT MAGAZINES

032c
www.032c.com

Clash Magazine
www.clashmusic.com

Dazed & Confused
www.dazeddigital.com

Esquire
www.esquire.com

Fantastic Man
www.fantasticman.com

GQ
www.gq.com

Halcyon
www.halcyonmag.com

Hypebeast
www.hypebeast.com

i-D
i-d.vice.com

Inventory
www.inventorymagazine.com

Kinfolk
www.kinfolk.com

Monocle
www.monocle.com

Pica-Post
www.pica-post.com

Proper
www.propermag.com

The Rig Out
www.therigout.com

ONLINE

5th St Bakery
www.5thstreetbakery.com

A Continuous Lean
www.acontinuouslean.com

Acquire
acquiremag.com

Being Hunted
www.beinghunted.com

BNTL
www.bntl.co.uk

Breaks Mag
breaksmag.com

Complex
www.complex.com

Four Pins
four-pins.com

Gear Patrol
www.gearpatrol.com

Grungy Gentleman
grungygentleman.com

Gwarizm
garywarnett.wordpress.com

Highsnobiety
www.highsnobiety.com

Hypebeast
www.hypebeast.com

It's Nice That
www.itsnicethat.com

Madbury Club
www.madburyclub.com

The Reference Council
www.thereferencecouncil.com

Selectism
www.selectism.com

The Selvedge Yard
selvedgeyard.com

Valet
www.valetmag.com

BRAND CONTACTS

18 Waits
www.18waits.com

Aether
www.aetherapparel.com

Aitor Throup
aitorthroup.com

Albam Clothing
www.albamclothing.com

Arc'teryx Veilance
veilance.arcteryx.com

Big John
www.bigjohn.co.jp

Billykirk
www.billykirk.com

Closed
www.closed.com

Common People
commonpeopleclothing.co.uk

Denim Demon
denimdemon.se

Deus Ex Machina
deuscustoms.com

Eastland
www.eastlandshoe.com

Eat Dust
eatdustclothing.com

Ebbets Field Flannels
www.ebbets.com

Engineered Garments
www.engineeredgarments.com

Filson
www.filson.com

Folk
www.folkclothing.com

Garbstore
www.couvertureandthegarbstore.com

Gilded Age
www.gildedagenyc.com

Gitman Bros.
gitmanvintage.com

Golden Bear
www.goldenbearsportswear.com

Grenson
www.grenson.co.uk

Howlin' by Morrison
www.morrison.be

Indigofera
www.indigoferashowroom.co.uk

Iron & Resin
www.ironandresin.com

Kelly Cole
kellycoleusa.com

Lavenham
www.lavenhamjackets.com

Left Field NYC
leftfieldnyc.com

Libertine-Libertine
libertine-libertine.com

Lightning Bolt USA
www.lightningbolt-usa.com

M.Nii
www.mnii.com

Maiden Noir
www.maidennoir.com

Mark McNairy
www.markmcnairy.com

Monitaly
www.monitaly.com

Muttonhead
www.muttonheadcollective.com

Naked & Famous Denim
nakedandfamousdenim.com

Nigel Cabourn
www.cabourn.com

Outlier
outlier.cc

Pike Brothers
pikebrothers.com

Publish Brand
publishbrand.com

Reigning Champ
www.reigningchamp.com

S.N.S. Herning
www.sns-herning.com

Stussy Deluxe
www.stussy.com/us/collections/deluxe

Tanner Goods
www.tannergoods.com

Tellason
www.tellason.com

The West Is Dead
www.thewestisdead.com

Universal Works
www.universalworks.co.uk

Wings + Horns
www.wingsandhorns.com

Won Hundred
www.wonhundred.com

Wood Wood
woodwood.dk

Yuketen
www.yuketen.com

ACKNOWLEDGMENTS

A sincere thank you to all the brands
and people who we worked with to make
this book happen. There are too many
to mention, but you know who you are.